One Step Beyond
A Teenage Odyssey in 1980s Los Angeles

By

Mike Pearson

Mike Pearson

The names and identifying characteristics of the individuals depicted in this memoir have been changed to protect their privacy.

Acknowledgements: Thank you so much to Robert Richards, Carlota Atlee and Jobe Benjamin for helping me with the art and editing of this book!

Missing Words Publishing

PO Box 2183

Manhattan Beach, CA 90267

First Printing March 2010

10 9 8 7 6 5 4 3 2 1

Copyright © 2010 Mike Pearson

All rights reserved. No parts of this book (except short quotes for reviews) may be reproduced or transmitted without permission of Mike Pearson.

Pearson, Mike.

One Step Beyond: A Teenage Odyssey in 1980s Los Angeles

Popular culture / memoir / music / 1980s / skateboarding / surfing / mod / punk rock / teenagers

All illustrations including cover and back by Robert Richards

Visit Robert E. Richard's website at: www.rerichardsart.com

Cover Design and illustrations photographed by Jobe Benjamin. Visit www.jobebenjamin.com

One Step Beyond

Contents

1. Winter 1981 - Smile You're Arrested
1. House of Gas Visited
1. Spring 1982 - The New Wave
1. Jeff, The Canyon and Vehicles Al Diablo
1. Girl Disturbed
1. Summer - Lords of Oil
1. Deep Summer - The Canyon Kid Men Of Rustic & Various Other Sick Puppies
1. Fall 1982 - This is the Modern World
1. Meet the Blaines
1. Violent Attack II, Too
1. Lights, Camera, Vomit
1. Eva
1. House of Fun
1. Winter - The Planet of the Apes
1. My Girlfriend Valerie
1. One Step Beyond
1. The Fat Lady Sings - Live at Boyola
1. The Beards
1. Afterward

Mike Pearson

One Step Beyond

Winter 1981

Smile, You're Arrested!

"Depression" by Black Flag

It was almost 1982 and my photographs were sitting in the developer taking too long to come out. My negative had been underexposed. I was a 12th grader and this was photo class. I enjoyed being in the darkroom, in my own world, breathing chemicals, dealing only with the images I chose. In the classroom area there were students congregating around the ratty couch in the back. They couldn't waste their valuable social time isolated in a darkroom, but I could. "Damn pictures, develop!" There it is. Finally! Ten minutes in the developer. It looked like I got some height off that jump, me on my motorcycle. I had just put a photo into the stop-bath when Mr. Savich, Vice Principal and Head of Security, walked into, and pulled me out of, the darkroom. Savich was a cheap suited, walkie-talkie clutching, defender of justice.

"Come with me," he said.

"Can I just get my photo into the fixer?"

"No. Come with me now!"

As I was being led out of there, I thought, what the hell is going on here? I didn't do anything! Taking me to the office ... for what? They're ruining my photos! We walked straight across the middle of the quad, with all the kids staring at me.

As we entered the admissions room in the front building I was shocked by what I saw. There were about fifteen kids in that room. They looked anxious, confused, nervous, and some actually looked angry. I was in the anxious and confused category. What the hell is going on? The principal and administrators were all there. There were three serious looking mustached men in suits whom I didn't recognize. It was quiet in there except for a couple of whispers among adults. I asked the kid next to me, "What's going on?" One of the mustache men turned his head and darted me a look. "Silence, please."

I stood there for thirty minutes, but it seemed much longer. A couple more kids were brought into the room during this time. Then they walked us outside where five police cars were waiting at the curb. They told me to put my hands in front of me and they snapped on a pair of handcuffs in what seemed like slow motion. I was stunned. This all seemed so wrong. My gut was wrenching. My face was blasted with heat. They put me in the back of one of the police cars along with two other kids. One of them was Kevin, who I knew fairly well. Sitting in the front of the car were two young, short-haired cops. We sat there for a few excruciating moments in silence. I looked over at Kevin. He had a disassociated look on his face that explained nothing. Then I asked the cops:

"Excuse me, sirs, but may I possibly inquire as to what I'm being arrested for?"

One of them turned around and looked me in the eye.

"You're being arrested for the sale of narcotics to a police officer."

Aaaggh! Kevin and I looked at each other; we were sickened. The other kid put his head down in his hands. "Bob?" Kevin said. We both realized that our friend of the last few months had been a narc. They drove us up to a church parking lot, which was on Sunset Boulevard just above the school. We pulled into the lot, and, sure enough, "Bob" was standing there. He wore a self-satisfied grin and leaned up against the black-and-white with his arms folded across his chest. He casually identified us by waving at us.

"Hi Kevin. Hi Mike. Hi Randy."

I wasn't even a drug dealer. In the ninth grade I used to sell people film-containers of pot (weed that I often grew at my house), which I'd sometimes dilute with parsley. By twelfth grade, I hadn't smoked weed for two years! I had already been through, and out, of my pot phase. I didn't like the effect of weed anymore. In eighth and ninth grade I used to smoke out regularly with my friends and go skateboarding and listen to Led Zeppelin and go to Westwood and people watch and play video games and watch movies. Then I began to dislike weed, because I would start acting weird supposedly, and too deep with my friends, and they would want me to "maintain" and stop being a "lightweight." It was too stressful and emotionally difficult getting high. More and more, when I was stoned, I felt nervous, self-conscious, inadequate and dumb. So I quit.

I had met "Bob" at the beginning of twelfth grade. He said he came from South Carolina. He had a thick southern accent. He hung out with our group at "nutrition" and lunch. "Nutrition"—that's a funny thing to call it; the only thing we would ever eat was sugar-soaked sweet rolls and chocolate milk! I knew Bob for a couple months before he ever even mentioned pot. He told me that he hadn't smoked weed for a long time and he missed it. He said that he missed hanging out with his old friends back in South Carolina and smoking weed. I considered him a friend. I never thought for a minute that he was a narc. Nobody did. He had befriended everyone well in advance of bringing up the subject of weed. I was gullible and I felt sorry for him because he was an outsider and new in town (especially with his un-cool, shaved-on-the-sides, narc haircut). He seemed lonely; he didn't have any real friends. I was kind of lonely. I hung out with a group of kids at nutrition and lunch, but I wasn't close to anyone. I didn't have any real friends either.

Bob had a '68 Dodge Charger, which I thought was really cool. It was a massive gas guzzling, polluting American pile of crap, ugly, beat up and primer grey. I should have known it was a police car. It was sputtering and running really bad, and I liked cars, so I offered to do a tune-up on it with him. The engine was so big. I felt it was a shame to have it sputtering around when it could potentially fly. "Bob, your car is a Charger—it needs to charge! I'll help you do a tune-up on it." I told him to go get the parts and we could work on it after school in the school's parking lot. I would help him change the spark plugs, wires, points, and I'd do the timing for him. As we worked on the car, Bob brought up how he missed smoking pot again.

I thought to myself, I do have that crap sitting up in my closet. A little bit of bad homegrown had been gathering dust up in my closet for about two years. I figured I'd just give it to Bob. The big mistake was that he held out a ten-dollar bill to me and I took it. If only I had insisted that it was a gift. He disappeared for a couple weeks after that and I didn't think anything of it. I went on, business as usual, being low profile at school, and riding my "enduro" dirt bike motorcycle with friends after school in an open dirt area at Temescal Canyon and up on the fire roads.

I had prided myself on not fitting in with the upper-middle-class Pacific Palisades environment. Kids at Pali were driving around in their dad-bought white Rabbit convertibles and new "Beemers," with their pink Ralph Lauren polo shirts with starched collars turned up and pleated pants and preppy Topsiders. Completing the uniform were Ray Ban Wayfarer sunglasses and cashmere sweaters tied around bronzed bulging volleyball necks. Sick, sick! I was embarrassed and disturbed. It was like Invasion of the Body Snatchers, and they were pumped up!

"What did you get on the SAT? Oh, you only got a 1500? My daddy would take away my beach club membership if I were that stupid. How are you ever going to be a billionaire and live in the Palisades with those loser scores! You've got two strikes against you. You're not only stupid, but you're ugly too! You'll never succeed!"

I didn't fit in with that aggressive mindset. My self-esteem was down and I didn't feel competitive. I was mostly bitter and irritated. The Palisades environment had always been cutthroat, but this was a particularly ruthless time. The seventies were over. A grueling new breed of Reaganite had replaced the good-time party hesher (hard-rock lovin' weed toker) of the '70s. These "agro gyros," as we used to call them, were hyper-focused on wealth, power, prestige and dominance. We called them "gyros," because, when they surfed, they got on waves and, instead of riding the wave, they had to gyrate so hard by going ballistic and kicking ass that they destroyed the wave. I could envision them later on in corporate jobs where they could keep gyrating, but on a scale where they could decimate the environment and things in their path in a much more substantial way.

One Step Beyond

Gone were the earlier days of Palisades parties where the kids were hippies, dancing carefree to sixties and seventies rock such as Steve Miller Band, The Band, the Dead, The Eagles, Janis Joplin, The Doors, etc. Pot was being replaced by cocaine, and Volkswagen bugs had been replaced by the most expensive motherfuckin' car a kid could get his hands on. Reagan and Rocky and Rambo were here now and were kicking some extreme ass for this country and getting us back in the driver's seat!

This was the era of conservative preppies. Tucker Carlson style. A lot of these kids didn't rebel against their parents; they already were their parents. I didn't like the preppies or the jocks. I couldn't have been a jock if I wanted to anyway; I wasn't any good at team sports. My dad never once threw me a ball. I don't know if I can blame that or my one bad eye, but I didn't have much hand-eye coordination. I was pretty good at skateboarding and surfing, though—the non-team sports, where I could do my own thing and not be responsible for letting others down if I screwed up. At school I hung out with surfers, musicians, freaks and geeks and video game addicts.

My family was kind of strange.

My mom was charming, but anxious, and talking non-stop. She was a Baptist who grew up dirt poor in east Texas. My dad was raised in an upper-middle-class Jewish Texan family. Both of their families lived in east Texas for about five generations. My mom and dad grew up in small towns about an hour away from each other, but they didn't meet until they had both been married once and divorced and were living in Los Angeles. They met at the dry cleaners where my mom worked. She was a dutiful housewife and did my dad's laundry before they even knew each other.

My mom had a lot of wild mood swings and intense feelings when I was a young kid, and I experienced it all. She didn't even attempt to keep her problems to herself. She unloaded her emotional baggage on me from the time I was old enough to look like I might understand the shit, from about five on. To me it was very stressful in my house. Over the years my dad increasingly withdrew from my mom emotionally and she became more and more desperate, angry and despondent over this abandonment. This was while I was in elementary. She pretty much gave up trying to reach him once I was in junior high.

My dad worked as a talent agent with old movie, TV and stage stars. When he came home he didn't want to deal with my mom or me and my brother and grandma. He didn't seem to know how to deal or to want to try to learn how. He sat in his chair and dove into his paper, TV and Johnny Walker. My mom wasn't getting her needs met by him anymore, emotionally and sexually. I was the container for her feelings from about ages five through eleven. She hadn't established any good friendships in which she could process or dump some of the anxiety and feelings. She talked my head off and I listened. I don't think she knew how inappropriate this was to burden a little boy with her marital frustrations and anxieties.

She was disassociated from her own childhood, which was ripped away from her at the age of twelve when her father died and her mother went to bed depressed. She had to become an adult immediately and get a job to support her mother, little brother and sister. Her mother was despondent, emotionally immature and childlike. My mom missed out on important portions of her childhood and became stunted as well. My grandmother had been a victim of emotional abuse by her mother and we suspected some sexual abuse by her father.

My mom as a child also had to deal with moving to a new town every six weeks because her father was a "wildcat" oil well driller. They were a bit like gypsies; he would get hired to drill wells way out in the country. She was a survivor who never stopped to consider what was appropriate. It was a free for all. It was all about seat-of-the-pants survival. I always felt my mom was a bit of a savage. In public my mom had pretty good manners most of the time. The savage part came out when things got rough.

It seemed like I was always trying to comfort her emotionally. This was out of empathy but also out of concern for my own well-being. I thought of her as pretty fragile; she had threatened suicide many times. My father never stepped in to save me from my mom's engulfment. I was very angry with him. I thought that he was selfish and glad that someone else was dealing with her so he wouldn't have to. Alcohol helped him avoid and deny the problems. On the other hand I felt sorry for my dad because I saw him as a weak man, physically, and as a father and husband. He had bad legs and clubfeet. He had a barrel chest and appeared much older than he was. He was 50 when I was born. On the positive side, he was a smart, interesting, sarcastic gruff-talking guy who was actually pretty gentle and vulnerable underneath it all. He also had interesting entertainer friends, like Buster Keaton, Pat O'Brien, Cyd Charisse, and Bob Crane, who would come around.

My younger brother, four years younger than I, was aligned with my father. When he was born my father told my mother, "Good, now there's one for me." The family had opposite teams. In the middle of the weird mix was my maternal grandmother, who always lived with us. She couldn't stand to be alone. My parents bought her a house but she refused to stay in it. She was a constant nag; she was filled with anxiety and was very negative and fearful. Sorry Grams. She meant well and could be kind and helpful when performing tasks, like making Kraft macaroni and cheese and running bath water and washing our hair in the sink. She meant well and did love us. But she was also the most intrusive person I had ever met. She would follow different people around the house. She had a dependent personality and no concept of boundaries or personal privacy. There was no lock on my room or bathroom and she would barge in at any time to tell me some important information, like that a plane just crashed or some other cheerful news. When the rest of us were out she spent her time sitting for hours just staring out the window. I feel sad sometimes when I think back on her life.

She and my mom were such intrusive people. These hillbillies never knew otherwise; they lived in one room shacks, and sometimes tents, growing up. They were all with each other 24/7, bathing in the same dirty water in the same room while telling themselves that they were lucky and grateful to have what little they had. They felt fortunate to have a roof over their heads and food and clothes, and to be able to go to school.

For me, food, clothes, education, and nice living was a given. I didn't even think about it. I had the luxury of taking those things for granted. What I was hungry for was to be listened to and supported from time to time. Instead, I was the one listening and supporting until I couldn't even see straight. A little privacy would have gone a long way too. I couldn't even have a wet dream without it being discovered and brought to my attention. My mom and grandma couldn't believe anything was wrong in our family because they felt so lucky to have what they had; we lived in a big house and had plenty of stuff. They didn't know much about a person's need for emotional sustenance.

It was an emotionally vacant childhood, filled with the best of material comforts. From the time I was twelve, (the same age as my mom when her dad died) I was on my own emotionally. At this point I started to stay away from the house a lot. I still felt obligated and responsible for my mom's emotional well being, so I would always be sure to come home and check on her and listen to her so I could relieve some of her anxiety and feelings. I was afraid that if I didn't offer some emotional support to her that she might make good on her threats to kill herself.

On the other side of things, my mom was funny, and caring, and cool in many ways. She would type my papers for me and drive my friends and me to skateboard parks. If I asked her to drive me somewhere she would always do it. She would buy me pretty much whatever I wanted. She and my dad were generous with money. I also knew that if I were ever in big trouble she would be there to help me.

She was a great storyteller and my friends loved her because she made them laugh and she was warmer and very accepting compared to most of their moms. In public she presented well. Her Texan accent would thicken as people became increasingly engaged with her humorous no-bullshit country anecdotes. My friends thought she was cool and didn't understand why I sat there steaming throughout her stories. There were two reasons: I was mad at her for being so self-involved and constantly needing attention (when I needed some too), and I didn't want to in any way encourage her telling any more stories, stories I had already heard a million times.

Here she goes again! I'd think. Oh my God! Heard it! I've heard it a thousand times! Will she just SHUT UP!

Example:

Mom: "And then Michael's father looked over and saw that the cat was hanging onto the roof of the car by the metal strip thingamajig, and we were still going about 40 miles an hour at this point, and all this was on the Coast Highway! Somehow that damn cat was on the roof of the car when I drove off and he got himself attached to the vinyl roof. I was about to turn into the beach parking lot and Michael's father was yelling "Severe Tire Damage! Severe Tire Damage!" I was screaming, "SHUT UP Severe Tire Damage!" "And Michael rolled down the window and pulled the cat inside the car. That was the last time I've seen that cat anywhere near my car. He's scared of the car. He won't go near it."

The biggest problem for me was that she never stopped talking and that nothing was off-limits. She talked to me about everything. She talked for years all about her frustration regarding my selfish and unavailable father. As a result, once I became a teenager I stayed away from the house as much as possible. I would come and go as I pleased. There were no rules or limits set for me. At fourteen I got into punk rock and started going to shows in Hollywood and Orange County on my moped. At fifteen, I got a motorcycle and I talked my parents into letting me drive their goofy blue AMC Hornet station wagon—without a license, I was too young! I went skateboarding, surfing, smoking pot, and motorcycle-riding all the time. I just had to be out of the house. Punk rock helped me get a more rebellious attitude and push away some of my sense of guilt and obligation about my mom.

I found out about punk in ninth grade, summer, 1979. I cut my hair short to one inch. At the time, 99% of people still had hair over their ears. Haircuts of the time were still related to the disco blow-dried, feather look. Short hair was rare and considered pretty strange and different. It had been almost fifteen years since people had had short hair. Only Travis Bickle of Taxi Driver, members of the armed services, brain surgery patients, and the rare punker had short hair.

I loved punk rock. At the shows I felt as though I was a part of something super exciting, revolutionary and modern. It was music that, at the time, most people couldn't understand or appreciate. Punk allowed me to be proud of feeling strange and different. I could now wear those feelings like a badge of honor.

Back then, I would ride my moped to the Hollywood and South Bay shows with my friend Pinsky on the back. We saw some of the greatest bands at their peak. The early punk shows were small, usually only 100 to 200 people or so. I'd guess there were only around 500 punk rock fans in Los Angeles in the late-seventies. It was a small scene and punk rockers had a look that was bizarre and scary to regular people. The level of energy at those shows is impossible to describe. People truly went ballistic and crazy, singing along, running and flailing, spazzing out, pogoing, jumping off 2nd story balconies and speaker cabinets and stuff. There was so much freedom and power in the music; it created the sense that anybody could play music in a band if they wanted. The energy between the bands and the audience made it so that everyone was creating a communal peak experience, not just the musicians. Punk rock eliminated the line between the audience and the stage. Everybody became the show. I loved how it was a big "screw you" to the old school of rock n' rollers who had spent so much time learning how to wheedle away pointlessly on leads. Punk said "hell no" to emulating the jerk off "Guitar Gods."

I also loved punk for the cathartic release. I was no longer alone with my anger and isolation. It was validating to me. It gave outsiders a place to come together and something to be a part of, reducing their feeling of alienation. In this scene, if you were weird you were appreciated and respected for it.

In the late seventies, all of the weird new music coming out was considered "punk." Oingo Boingo, the B52s, the Cars, Talking Heads, and Blondie were called punk just because it was so different. None of these bands were big in America yet; it was too early for them. People didn't get it. People understood the Eagles, Led Zeppelin, Boston, Foreigner, Foghat, Styx, Bad Company, ACDC, and Aerosmith. What wasn't there to understand about that? Party, party, get laid, get laid, get stoned, and worship the rock stars.

Punk was one of the things in my life that made me feel good. But I drifted away from it by the 11th grade because I didn't want to hang out with Pinsky anymore; he was becoming increasingly reckless with sex, violence and drugs.

One Step Beyond

I was scared to be around him. I thought something bad might happen if I continued to hang around him. He was cutting himself, giving himself "Germs burns" with cigarettes, having sex with weird skanky 25 year olds. I spent a year or so mostly surfing and taking it easy with a couple friends. It was strange that I would be busted for drugs now that I was a more mellow and law-abiding person than I had been for years. I guess it was a delayed karmic reaction.

The first quarter of twelfth grade went by. Bob hadn't been around for two weeks, and I hadn't even thought about him. Then, out of nowhere, came the bust. I was arrested five days before my seventeenth birthday.

My parents believed the lame story I told them. I said that I saw a pot plant growing down the street in the traffic island and picked it for lonely Southern Bob. I said I felt sorry for Bob, which was true. I told them some neighborhood burner must have planted the weed there and I just grabbed it. I got the idea because I planted weed there a couple years back.

The truth was that the pot was mine and had been sitting in my closet from when I was a ninth-grade stoner. It was weak homegrown and not really worthy of being smoked.

My parents didn't argue with my story. They just took it; it was easier that way. For a day or so they were disturbed about my arrest but they quickly minimized it. Within a day they acted as if nothing had happened. This made me feel sad and extremely lonely. My feeling was: I get arrested and that doesn't even get me attention! I was hurting. My mom and dad did care, but neither of them knew how to deal with strong feelings of helplessness. Happy feelings were cool, but negative scary feelings were too terrifying and meant to be crammed swiftly up one's ass.

My parents got me a lawyer and I went to court. My lawyer got the charges dropped after arguing "entrapment." Then my mom went down and tried to use some of her past PTA president clout to talk the principal into letting me stay at Pali. It didn't work. He told us that I had to go to a different school.

I went to Venice High. I couldn't believe I had to go to Venice. It was either Venice or Hamilton. I hadn't even heard of Hamilton so I picked Venice. I would have liked Santa Monica High (I knew a couple kids from there). But they wouldn't let me go there because one of the other kids who was busted already had first dibs on it. That kid was the only kid who could qualify as an actual drug dealer out of all the kids who were busted, and he got the first choice of schools. That pissed me off. They wouldn't let me go there, too, because they figured we'd start a drug cartel.

Going to Venice was hard. I was very depressed but not too aware of it; I just kept plodding along. Venice was only seven miles down the coast, near the beach like the Palisades, but that was where the similarities ended. Venice had gangs and tough kids. It was so unlike the homogeneous affluent white Palisades.

My first week there, I was walking along between some bungalows and I encountered two aspiring cholo thugs. They tried in an unconvincing way to get me to give them money.

"Hey, short hair, where are you going? Why don't you give us some money?"

One Step Beyond

I gave them a strained smile and kept on walking. I think the kids there thought I was a nerd because my hair was short. They didn't get it! I wasn't GQ, an Army weirdo, or a football jock, and no, I didn't have a brain operation! It was none of those. I wasn't a geek for Christ's sake!

Didn't they know my hair stood for something? Punk rock!

What? My statement wasn't working? My statement was too vague?

Maybe I was too subtle a punk rocker.

I was nauseated that it was 1982 and the Venice guys were still into hesher rock: Ozzy Osbourne, Iron Maiden, and The Scorpions, etc. Many of these guys wore their hair well below the ears, feathered, parted in the middle, and sported weird half-ass mustaches.

One of the things that surprised me about Venice was I didn't see many beautiful girls. I kept looking for them and didn't see them. It wasn't like Pali, where half the girls looked like Miss Teen USA. That kind of caught me off guard. Another surprising thing was that girls at Venice got so much more attention from the guys than the girls did at Pali. At Pali, the guys tried to be cool, play games, and ignore them. At Venice the guys didn't even attempt restraint. Maybe the over-the-top drooling-like-an-idiot approach worked. I wasn't sure. I was confused about how socializing was supposed to work. I just stood around alone, feeling displaced, on the outside looking in.

A guy would approach a girl and say, "Hey, baby, wanna sit on my face?" and start laughing, "Huh-huh, huh-huh-huh," snickering, giggling, and drooling. I was disgusted and amazed all at once.

It amazed me that many of the girls actually liked the approach. What did they care? It was attention. Like a ticker tape in my head, the knowledge that I was depressed and isolated, kept rolling like some kind of bad after school special. If I could only shut the movie off, I could quit trying to understand the environment and join in with the other idiots and have some fun. But I was just too serious, and I didn't know how to fit in or trust anyone. I couldn't be light and joke around with people, I wasn't able, and I was lost.

During my time at Venice I just kept to myself. Every day during lunch I would just go to my car and listen to music. One day I went out there and found my window broken and my stereo gone; wires were spilling out of the dash. Life had become tedious and unbearable. I hadn't had any fun in so long. I just seemed to be waiting for something good to happen. I didn't know if it would happen or how to make it happen. I was stuck. Seventeen and feeling like life was just a big burden. I thought a few times about offing myself but figured that if there were reincarnation I'd probably end up back a bunch of steps from where I was now. I didn't like the thought of that. I just kept going.

In January of 1982, I had a meeting with my parents and the probation officer. I had another hearing coming up. They were going to decide whether to end probation or not. He said that I should get some kind of job so I would seem more like a regular kid and not like a drug dealer. I figured it would be good for me to have to do something. Everything began to look up once I started working at the gas station.

House of Gas Visited

"(Dawning of a) New Era" by The Specials

I knew Eddie because he was my friend Mark Wilson's mom's boyfriend. Eddie worked at the gas station at the beach. When I was at Mark's house, Eddie would often be talking about things that happened at the gas station. It sounded like a fun place to work.

I went by Mark's to talk to Eddie about getting a job there. Eddie was drinking Heineken and watching the Lakers with Magic Johnson killing their opponents. I decided to wait till the commercial break to talk to Eddie.

"Hey, Ed-man, is that a pretty cool job working down there? Do you think I should try to get a job down there?"

Eddie spoke extremely slowly, in a Californian accent, separating all his syllables.

"Yeah, Mike-man. It's killer. What more can you ask? On the beach, there're babes everywhere. You'll dig it."

Eddie was a laid-back guy. Twenty-eight years old, 5' 9", with longish, brown, wavy thinning hair, sort of roly-poly, a beer-gut, but a strong friendly hell-raiser kind of guy. Eddie liked to talk a lot. He wasn't much for listening. Friendly and as casual as hell but somehow it seemed that he was sitting on a bunch of anxiety.

"How much does it pay?" I asked. The game comes back on so I wait till the next break and ask again.

"How much does it pay?"

"Well, man, it starts out at $3.35. But it's cool! Just come down and talk to Klaus.

Bart Wilson, Mark's fifteen-year old brother, walked through the room, giving a look of dread upon hearing the word "Klaus."

"Ugh ... Klaus," Bart moaned.

"What?" I turned and asked Eddie, nervously. "What's the matter? What's Klaus like?"

"Klaus's cool, you just got to get to know him. At first, man, he's like a Nazi; but that's just Klaus, man; that's his trip."

"He's cool if you like Nazis!" Bart said.

A week later, I got up the nerve to go to the gas station to talk to Klaus. My house was on a cliff overlooking the ocean a couple blocks north of the gas station. It was a three-minute drive by car, or a fifteen-minute walk. The Pacific Coast Highway and its endless speedway of cars separated the gas station from the beach. You had to walk through a tunnel to get to the beach from the gas station or you risked the chance of getting hit by a car (there were no crosswalks). I was more afraid to talk to Klaus than to cross PCH in a wheelchair.

I took comfort in the fact that Eddie would be there. That would make it a little easier. Everything I had heard about Klaus made me uncomfortable. Eddie said that he had put in a good word for me and that everything was cool with Klaus.

One Step Beyond

That made me feel a little better too. I slowly approached Klaus's hideous little office. Heinous, I thought. The walls were supposed to be white, but they weren't; they were stained a sickening yellow from years of cigar and cigarette smoke.

Klaus was sitting there at his dirty little gray desk, smoking a cigar and counting stacks of money and credit card slips. Klaus went on and on with his business. He had to know I was there. I was two feet away.

He knew I was there but he kept ignoring me. He was counting money and puffing away on his cigar, and he couldn't be distracted. What the hell was this guy's story?

Klaus was late-fifties, a tough, round guy, about 5'10", had a gut, was stocky, and looked strong, like maybe he could kick your ass. By his posture, he looked like he might have been a boxer back when he was young. Actually, he was. His shoulders rode a little high like a boxer defending himself. He had become a bit old, though, and his hair was gray and there wasn't much of it anymore, and it was the kind of hair that flitted around in different directions when the wind blew. I waited there, patiently, not wanting to piss him off, because he looked like the easily enraged type.

Finally I said, "Uh ... hi."

He peeked up at me, grimacing, eyes squinting, then he said in a long, slow disgusted German accent:

"What? What the fuck do you want?"

"Uhh ... A job?" I said clumsily.

"Why the fuck do you wanna work here?" he blurted out hostilely.

Then he started shaking his head in disgust: "You don't need a job. You're rich! You don't need any money. We don't need any more ahsoles here! Go home! We don't need you." "But..." "You wouldn't last a minute around here. You would be so fucked up after a week you wouldn't even know what to do. You wouldn't even last a fucking second around here!"

"But..." I added.

"Go!" he pointed to the door.

"But, but..."

"Go!" he pointed, more adamantly.

"But ... but..."

"GO!"

"What's the big deal?" I blurted out, standing my ground. "I can handle it! I need the money."

"Yeah, right, Ahsole. You don't need the fucking money."

I stood there, staring at him, trying to calm myself down, thinking:

"This guy's out of his fucking mind! What an asshole! And it's not 'ahsole, its ASSHOLE!'"

I was just staring at Klaus, baffled as to why the hell I was still even standing there.

I was just about to walk away in defeat when he said, "All right. I'll give you a try. But if you can't handle it, after a couple of days, you go."

"Okay," I said, but thought to myself: "Finally. What a jerk! Let me the fuck out of this place!"

The night before I started at Klaus's, I went over the preparation materials he had given me. It was a kit that had some tapes and was entitled: "The Chevron Experience."

Klaus loaned me the tapes and made it more than clear that he wanted them back, telling me over and over not to keep "the fucking tapes."

The tapes were old and all about:

"No Ma'am." "Yes Ma'am."

"Yes, sir-ee. Would you like your tire treads licked clean? Have a nice day."

The newer updated version would be like:

"Yeah, I guess you can use the squeegee—but don't steal it, motherfucker."

"No, we don't have a crack machine."

"You're being stalked? No hiding in this gas station."

"Full serve? Fuck you."

The old version:

"Ma'am, may I check under your hood, please?"

I studied the manual carefully. I was prepared. I put my seventeen-year-old self into one of those blue-striped gas station shirts and dark blue pants and hit the pumps.

There, propped up and hanging over the oil case, was the skinny atrophied-muscle dude I'd be working with. Dirk. I introduced myself to Dirk. When I shook his hand it was so limp it felt like I grabbed an old slimy open-faced processed chicken sandwich. Dirk was from Santa Monica. No offense to Dirk, but he happened to be the laziest, burned-out, whining motherfucker I'd met in a long time.

Dirk stood around a lot complaining. Complaining, whining, and leaning against the oil case. Complaining and whining. He was one of the people who over the years contributed to the wearing down of paint on the oil case, from all of the leaning and whining.

I would soon become one of those people.

His posture was bad. His shoulders sat there way too far forward. His hair hadn't been cut in eight months and was long and greasy. His pants were falling down.

Dirk started me off by giving me some important information.

"Klaus is such an asshole. Klaus is such a dick. Klaus fucking this, Klaus fucking that. That fucking Klaus, fuck that Klaus."

"That fucking Nazi German jack-off. Klaus is such a fucking dick!"

He also gave me some more data:

"Rod is such a fucking dick asshole."

And to give Dirk some credit, he was right about that one. Rod was a fucking dick asshole. Rod was the gas station's big overweight slob mechanic—'70s-style, a big mustache, and he was really mean. His pants were too big and low, and you didn't want him to get down on one knee to look at a tire or something, because you'd be getting a good look at a fat, hairy butt crack. Quintessential '70s California redneck.

His pride and joy was his fixed-up, red, valley-mobile Mustang. It was jacked-up with huge tires on the back.

I believed what Dirk said about Klaus, too. Klaus did seem like a Nazi. Dirk said he kept an eight-by-ten glossy of Adolph in his office drawer and he would pull it out every now and then to worship it.

I'd only worked there for a week and already Klaus was driving me crazy. He always had some kind of critical jerk comment for me:

"Why did you do that, Michael?"

"What the fuck are you putting that there for?"

"Is it necessary we change everything for you, Michael, now that you come here? Do we have to do that? Do we? Do we?"

"Michael you are such a fuck-up. Oh, I should have never given you a chance. I should've known you couldn't handle it."

One more week of constant criticism went by and I finally couldn't take it anymore and I blew up at Klaus. And that seemed to be just what he was waiting for the whole time. It wasn't anything more obnoxious than usual; it was just the last-straw.

"Michael, don't use any more of those rags. They cost me a fucking fortune to get cleaned. You don't have to use—"

"Look," I said, "I can't do anything right around here—I'm sorry! I just can't take this shit any longer! I try so fucking hard to do this all right. But there is no way to please you! Forget it! This is the worst. Impossible! Forget this.

One Step Beyond

You're a nightmare! This isn't worth it. This sucks! I quit!" I threw down my little red rag on the concrete.

Klaus just stared at me in amazement. He couldn't believe it; he couldn't believe I said that shit to him. I guess he'd never been talked to like that. He looked completely dumbfounded. He was staring at me intensely. I thought he might even punch me. Then I noticed he was trying really hard to fight back a grin; then a giant smile formed all over his face.

It was like he was thinking: "You fucking asshole!" But he loved me from that point on.

Then he said calmly, "Okay, Michael, we'll give you a second chance. Okay. We were just trying to tell you a couple things."

I didn't know whether I wanted to dance with this man or murder him.

The next day I was at the pumps and Klaus came out of his office and walked up to me.

"Man," he said. "You really gave me shit. Man, you really gave me shit the other day. I couldn't believe it. You really fucked me up, Michael. You really fucked me up."

I started grinning a little; then I said, "What? No, I didn't."

"Oh, yes. You really gave me shit the other day," he said.

Then he called over to Dirk. Dirk was leaning against the pump.

"Didn't Michael really give me shit the other day? You remember that. I could not believe how much shit he gave me. He really let me have it."

Dirk grunted, "Yeah."

Then Klaus turned to me and smiled and said:

"Nobody has ever told me off like that before. You ahsole! You are such an ahsole, Michael."

Then he walked away. I knew he really liked me after that. Klaus and I were good friends from that point on. After that he just brought up constructive criticism when necessary.

I guessed Klaus respected me for not taking his crap. I was figuring out that a lot of people don't really like it when you take their shit. It allows them to be an asshole, and who really wants to feel like an asshole. I was learning that one way to get respect from people is to not take their shit.

I began to understand Klaus. Klaus had been in business for a long time. Over the years he had developed a very specific way of doing things, a way in which things seemed to work. He knew what had to be done for just about any problem that might come up. He had been through all of it over the last twenty years, and he didn't like hassles, so he was a nitpicker.

Either you got into that mentality, or were driven crazy by it.

Another thing I knew about Klaus was that he would probably be lost or depressed if he didn't have the gas station. He secretly liked it, maybe even loved it. Eddie did too. Their lives focused mainly on the gas station.

One Step Beyond

It was easy for Klaus to comprehend life revolving around a gas station, practically living at a gas station, because that's exactly what Klaus had been doing for the past twenty years, since 1962.

Klaus's life and his gas station had somehow become one. This wasn't so bad for Klaus. It never got boring, it wasn't a painful life, and it wasn't even a hard life. Work was outdoors at the beach. It was a good life, compared to many. The Pacific Ocean sat right there across Pacific Coast Highway. It was cliché California beautiful right there on the other side of Klaus's ugly little one-way-mirror money counting window.

On a Saturday after getting off work from the station I decided to go by the Wilsons' house and visit Eddie and whoever else was there. They lived a block from the beach.

I saw Eddie working on his speedway motorcycle in the glassed-in '70s rec room. Then I saw Bart's mom, Sandy, in the window of her kitchen. She stuck her head out and said in her Boston accent:

"So I hear you're one of Klaus's Gestapo agents now?"

"Yep, he's got me working pretty hard. What a way to make a living."

Sandy was super nice and very down to earth. We would always call her by her first name, which was really different for me. On my street, growing up, families were old fashioned and conservative, and it was, "Hi, Mrs. Delaney. Hi, Mrs. Goode, etc." I had never called anyone's mom by her first name before.

And Eddie was more like one of us than any kind of dad role model. He was actually more of a nutcase than we were.

He raced speedway motorcycles. That's really a crazy sport. The motorcycles have no brakes, because they weigh too much or some shit like that, and the bikes are designed to go in only one direction, really fast, on a circular dirt track. About thirty guys are on these weird-looking motorcycles, and they're sliding around the track sideways, and if somebody crashes (which is all the time), they either embed themselves into a hay bale or get run over repeatedly by everyone behind them. Eddie said he was going to retire from speedway soon. I think it took a lot out of him being run over all the time.

I walked into the rec room, sliding the big glass door shut behind me.

"Hey Edder."

"Hey, Mike-man, hold this wrench right here while I put this chain on."

The motorcycle was balanced on a blue plastic milk crate. Eddie was always working on that thing. What on earth could be so wrong with it? Sandy's linoleum was all greasy.

That week Eddie had instantly become the mechanic at Klaus's because Rod Asshole was fired. Hallelujah. He was such a jerk. I wondered what had happened. I also wondered how much Eddie knew about fixing cars.

"So Eddie, why did Rod get fired?"

"Just between you and me," he made me lean forward, and then he said in a conspiratorial tone, "it was because he aimed his butt-crack at too many customers."

I could always expect something like that from Eddie. I could never get a straight answer from him. It was kind of like asking my dad a question. My dad wouldn't answer with a joke, but the answer would be to a question I never asked. For instance, if I asked (referring to a football game on TV):

"Dad, why did that guy just throw the ball when he could've run?" He'd say:

"Jim Thorpe was the greatest athlete who ever lived."

I asked Eddie another question:

"So, now that you're the mechanic, are you going to be able to pull off most of the repairs?"

"Mike-man, can monkeys whack off?"

"Well, yeah, I guess they can."

I knew Eddie didn't have any formal training, but now he was going to do all the repairs on the cars. If he got stuck, though, Klaus would be there to help him. Klaus knew a lot about cars from when he was young in Germany; he was a certified Mercedes mechanic there. For the past couple weeks I watched Eddie fix cars and everything was basically trial and error. Error first, and then a trial with Klaus about what went wrong.

"Eddie, ahsole," Klaus would say. "What did you fuck up now? Do I have to do everything myself?"

I continued helping Eddie as he struggled with the motorcycle.

"Mike, man, hold that wheel still," Eddie said. "I appreciate your help but you're jiggling that shit all over the place. To be a mechanic you have to be patient and take it easy."

"I am patient, too patient. You're taking forever."

Eddie and Sandy were a cool couple. He was in his late-twenties, and she was in her mid-forties. They had been together four years. They met at the grocery store. I got to know their family in the seventh grade soon after I met Mark while taking the bus to junior high together. Sandy and her kids moved to L.A. after she divorced Mark's dad a couple years back.

I was baffled because they seemed more Californian than my family, maybe because they were younger. They were definitely '70s-style beach people, except for Mark's younger brother, Bart, who was a pale and pasty computer kid who never went outdoors.

Then Mark walked by, flipping his perfectly straight, shoulder-length, hair out of his eyes. I waved and said, "Hey, Mark," and he waved ever so slightly by rotating his wrist once toward me. He had a strange tight-lipped angry smile. I wouldn't be stopping by Mark's room to visit him. We were no longer friends. We had a falling out in the ninth grade. He and my other friends dumped me at the time because of ninth grade peer politics of cool.

I couldn't believe that Sandy smoked pot and that she let Mark grow it in the house and smoke it whenever he wanted. As I mentioned before, the ninth grade had been my pot phase. The liberal Wilson policy, and my parent's see no evil, smell no evil, denial and neglect, made getting high easy, and possibly necessary. Having basically no guidance, no rules, and no supervision, we turned into little self-governed stoned freaks.

We would go around Mark's house collecting joint roaches from the ashtrays. Then we'd assemble them all into one big doobie. They always had these roaches around, usually sitting in the ashtrays around the pool table in the rec room. The guesthouse consisted of the rec room and Mark's bedroom. The guesthouse looked like a giant aquarium, big glass windows and sliding glass doors. Mark had it to himself most of the time, except when Eddie was using it as a lube-bay.

I finished helping Eddie with the wheel and said goodbye.

"See ya at the station, Edder."

"Yeah, Mike-man, see ya at the station."

Life was getting better now. High school was nearly over, a couple more months. The gas station was a cool place to be, at the beach, beautiful, light and flowing, and open. Things were changing and improving. I could feel it.

Mike Pearson

Spring 1982
The New Wave
"Don't You Want Me Baby" by The Human League

Dirk, the whiner, had quit. No more constant complaining. Spring was here. The weather was getting nice, and the beach was starting to come alive. We needed more workers. Klaus hired two new guys, Tony and Andre.

Tony was a charming, mischievous, boyish Latino 20-year-old who had the annoying habit of singing that Human League song "Don't You Want Me Baby?" constantly. I remember feeling fascination every time I heard that song, because it signaled a major change in music. It was the first "New Wave" song to be played on dinosaur-rock radio station KMET, which finally died because it resisted new music until the last minute but by then it was too late. It was sad because KMET started out with cutting-edge rock during the sixties but became paralyzed by its fear of upsetting its audience which had become older and set in their ways. KMET listeners were inhospitable to New Wave. Your typical handlebar-mustache thirty-year-old was heard screaming:

"What is this pussy music? Punk's bunk! Fucking weirdos. They're fags. It's just not right!"

But new wave cried out to them: "Don't You Want Me, Baby." Whether they liked it or not, this was the new shit, the new sound, the new wave. Tony had been a devoted KMET listener but couldn't find any reason to be reactionary about Don't You Want Me, Baby. To Tony, chicks dug Human League's Don't You Want Me Baby. And if they dug it, he did too, because he dug chicks.

On Tony's first day, I was working with him and he snapped my ass with a red oil rag and started singing:

"Don't you want me, baby?"

"Not really, dude," I said.

"So you live around here?" Tony asked.

"Yeah," I said. "I live right on top of that hill," pointing up to the right.

"You live up there? A rich kid, huh?"

"Uh, I don' know," I mumbled. Where do you live?" I asked.

"I live in Santa Monica. Let's say ... in the affordable section," and he laughed. "I live right next to the fucking freeway. All day and all night, Brrrrrrr, Brrrrrrr, cars."

He laughed again, seeming a little too happy.

"It used to be a nice neighborhood, but then they decided to run the freeway through it. They had to go south until they found the Mexican neighborhood, then they ran it through."

"Really, you think that's what they did?"

"You don't see a freeway right here, do ya? In Pacific Palisades? I don't think so."

One Step Beyond

"I don't think this is a very good place for the freeway," I said.

"Of course it isn't, Mr. Pacific Palisades. You're in charge."

He was right. Wealthy Westsiders had their way. Los Angeles harbor was originally planned for Santa Monica Bay (right in front of the gas station, actually) but Westsiders got it moved to Long Beach. They didn't want all that shit right there. Around the turn of the century there was a mile-long wharf just north of the gas station, where a railroad ran out to large ships. They got rid of the ships and tore that down, but the big rocks they left on the sand was our Jetty. That's the point break where we surfed. The waves peeled perfectly right off it. "The Jetty was pumping yesterday, dude," was the beginning of many a conversation among young dudes.

"No way!"

"Yeah, you fucking missed it. Me and Tad were getting stand-up dry barrels."

Yeah, right.

We felt lucky to live in the Palisades with its ocean full of endless exaggerated dry barrels. It was a nice place, and it looked like no one was going to fuck with it, not even Shell Oil, who wanted to do some oil drilling on the cliffs near my house. A Palisades organization full of lawyers called "No Oil" put a stop to that. The only thing that looked like it would change the Palisades for the worse was that it was becoming increasingly rich and anal and uptight. Fences and gates were going up everywhere.

A paranoid Palisades resident on the phone with Mac Guard security forces says:

"I thought I saw a black person."

In four seconds, ten patrol cars pull up with wanna-be cops making five bucks an hour. They all hop out, fumbling for their weapons, scared as hell.

The accused perpetrator raises his hands in the air.

"Goddammit, I go to the Bahamas for two weeks and get myself a tan ... "

"Oh, I'm sorry, Mr. Meadowdale. We didn't ... We're just ..."

That was the Palisades.

Andre came to work at the gas station a week after Tony. Andre was a skinny, funky, black dude from South L.A. He used a lot of slang. Half the time I didn't know what the hell he was talking about. Both Tony and Andre were pranksters. They were always joking around. They hit the gas station like monsters in a Japanese sci-fi movie.

"So Mike," Andre said. "You live around here? This shit is nice. You've got some beautiful women around here. A rich boy like you must get laid a lot."

"Yeah right, all the time ... like once."

"I may not have a lot of money, but I'll tell you I have the most beautiful Portuguese wife and baby. Have you ever fucked a Portuguese woman, Mike?"

"No, can't say that I have. You have a baby? How old are you?"

"I'm 33."

"You look a lot younger than that."

One Step Beyond

"Why, thank you. That's nice of you, Mike."

When I really looked close, though, I could tell by his wrinkles and his tired face that he was a bit older than you might think from a distance, but boy, was he immature. Andre was always jabbering on, bragging about his gorgeous Portuguese wife and his child. I was never sure if he was telling the truth about them. Did they really exist? I never actually saw them, but I saw lots of other women with Andre.

If he did have the so-called wife, he cheated on her, oh, as often as possible.

There were an extreme variety of women coming in to see Andre. They were all different colors and were from many different countries, but they all had one thing in common. They were nuts.

One day one of them went Fatal Attraction on him.

A Swede sped into the station in her beat up Japanese car crying out frantically: "Where's Andre!!!" Then she and Andre went off to the back to have some screeching conversation by the oilcan storeroom. I could see that Andre had the ability to push an already fragile psyche right off the edge.

Andre would try to get together with anything and everything that moved, no matter how insane. Tony was a tad more selective. Tony had a serious girlfriend as well. But that didn't stop him from picking up on women. It didn't even slow him down.

Both of them would flirt and tease women like crazy, even the most psychotic bag-women prostitutes imaginable. I'm talking insane women with a capital I, schizophrenic women that had makeup running down all over their faces.

Andre would give them compliments with total conviction. He wanted to get some.

"Hey Baby, you are looking mighty fine today. You have such a nice ass. You are just the type of girl I love to love. I want you to have my baby, baby."

Tony and Andre would write up credit slips to borrow money from the cash register so they could purchase blowjobs that were performed in the back room next to the greasy sink and oil cases.

A messed up woman comes in saying she needs money, "Bad, right now," and then either Tony or Andre would end up taking her into the oil storeroom in back. Blowjobs for twenty bucks!

I couldn't believe it! My innocent mind was now corrupted by this reality. I would watch them disappear into the oil-room with big cheesy smiles plastered across their faces, swinging their hips like disco maniacs, with thumbs up.

And I would be out amongst the pumps covering for them, filling up the cars, attending to everybody, while they were getting their weenies attended to. Then they would slowly waltz out of the back room swinging their arms like, "Hey!" with big relieved looks on their faces. Then they'd go and write up a credit slip so it could be deducted from their paychecks.

Blow jobs on credit!

And Tony had a lot of wise sayings, too:

"Drop the drawers and I'm yours."

A woman pulled up to get gas and they would smile and he'd start flirting by saying stuff like,

"Sure, I'd be happy to fill you up," then giving her a big wink.

Or: "Yes, you need to be pumped, baby—you do."

Or Tony might say to Andre:

"You get the windows ... I'll pump her."

They had only been working there for a couple weeks when Goldie Hawn drove up in her black Porsche. She was wearing dark sunglasses. They both scrambled for her. I just watched and listened while I did another car's windows.

Andre put in the gas, while Tony washed the windshield. Tony started flirting with her:

"Take off your glasses for a minute. I want to make sure you're not stoned." And she pulled her glasses down and smiled and politely said, "I'm not stoned. You're the one who's stoned."

She was right. He was. Andre and Tony were always stoned. They would smoke out about three times a day on the right side of the station in this little space where Klaus kept a bunch of old tires and the trash dumpster.

Tony lied with a big smile, "I'm not stoned."

Then he pointed to Andre: "He's the one who's stoned."

Andre said friskily, with his hand on the gas pump,

"I'm not stoned. I just get high off of sex! That's the only drug I need."

At this point, Goldie might have been thinking, "Goodbye Chevron ... Hello Shell."

Goldie was not singled out because of her celebrity status. These guys were not discriminating about whom they harassed—they harassed them all.

By now, I was starting to become familiar with all the regular customers.

Shadoe Stevens would come in, but we only knew him as Fred Rated—the guy on commercials for Federated electronic stores. He would come by about five times a week to use our payphone and get gas. He would use our phone every time he pulled in. Whom was he calling? I guess he was pretty popular and busy.

Life before cell phones! How did we survive?

Fred would be over at the pay phone at the end of the parking lot, and Andre would yell over at him:

"Fred R.! You the man! You cool! My stereo broke and shit, you get me a new one?"

Fred R. was like, "Okay, okay, be quiet. I'm on the phone."

Fred R. couldn't hear because there wasn't a phone booth anymore. They took it out a month ago and put in the new standard: a phone on a stand. No more booths where you could close the door, shutting yourself in, shutting out the noise. Gone was the old school American phone booth. Too much vandalism, I suppose and too expensive to clean. I was sad to see phone booths disappear.

Times were changing so fast. L.A. was changing. There were no longer two or three gas stations at every intersection. Mini-malls were popping up in their place now. These were an early-'80s phenomenon, the ones on corners invariably painted pink.

One positive change for L.A. was that smog was decreasing. There were now fewer stage-one smog alerts, and when you popped over the hill into the valley you wouldn't be assured of finding a thick blanket of brown smog sitting there. Cars were getting smaller and more efficient.

It was the eighties now all right. But there were still a few people living in the seventies; the seventies had only been over for a couple years now, and some people weren't ready to leave the decade behind.

Like our most hated customer.

Mutato Fingers pulled into the driveway. He took the driveway too fast as usual and his big black Lincoln rocked sideways and bounced up the incline before skidding to a halt in self-serve. The driver's door opened and out came this big hotshot jerk trying to look like a '70s Elvis businessman, with his gray pinstriped vest and black flared pants and big furry sideburns. For this guy, everyday was a matter of convincing himself that he was the greatest man who ever walked the earth. His car looked kind of like a limo. It was huge. And he looked kind of like a limo driver, with the black vest and polyester clothes. Klaus had known this guy for years. The guy always got out of his car and walked around, all tough-like, pulling up his pants, sticking his gut out, stretching, and taking a good look around. This day was no exception. What a hot shot.

He always had the same routine.

"Fill it up," he'd say, without bothering to even look at us. "And check everything."

Then he'd go to the bathroom (you wouldn't want to go in there for at least an hour after he was in there). Then he'd go talk to Klaus for about thirty minutes. We couldn't wait for him to leave because the thing about him was he was extremely rude.

He had pulled into self-serve and was ordering us around like a tyrant! Klaus would let him get away with it. Klaus said it was because he'd been a customer for a long time.

He always had us do extra little tasks.

"Hey, empty my ashtray, while you're at it."

After we served him he'd tell us what a shitty job we did.

"You guys really do a half-ass shitty job."

And this guy thought he was so cool 'cause he wore lots of polyester. At the time, polyester was anything but cool.

Then he would drive away and never say thank you. Not only that, but on top of it all he would complain to Klaus saying what a bad job we did. And he knew we hated him. We did what he said, Andre and Tony and I, but since it was impossible to please the bastard, we'd always do it with complete and total hatred. It was pretty funny. We'd give him really evil looks when he'd ask us to do stuff.

Somewhere deep inside, he may have wished that we'd get to know him and find out he was not such a bad guy after all. NO such luck!

That big Elvis-looking motherfucker had only three fingers on one hand. Three mutated fingers. We had no idea how they got like that, but it didn't make us dislike him any less. He got treated just like any other jerk.

One Step Beyond

Andre and Tony would fantasize aloud about stabbing his crusty claw with their Chevron pens, as he'd reach out to sign the credit card slip.

"Could you do the windows again," he'd say. "Look at that shitty job. You missed a spot. Jesus!" Then he'd point to a spot the size of an ant.

Or he'd say: "You better not let any gas run over onto the car like you did last time. I'll tell Klaus and you'll be out of a job!"

"Go ahead, Mutato Fingers!" we nearly screamed.

Elvis talked to Klaus about us, but Klaus paid no mind, because he knew the guy was a pain in the ass.

Another one of our usual customers was this chubby old round man. He drove a dark green Plymouth Scamp and wore a cowboy hat. He had thin, gray, stringy hair streaming out of the hat. This old bolo-tie cowboy always had me check everything on his car, too, absolutely everything, every time. A week after I checked everything, I would check everything again and nothing would ever be low. Transmission and power steering fluid doesn't go down after a week or even a month, or sometimes a year!

But I guess that's why the cheapskate's Scamp was still running like brand new after thirty-seven years. To top it all off, he always gave me one lousy quarter after checking his whole car, but he would never say thank you. He would never talk or smile, he would just hand me that measly quarter.

No quarter was ever going to pay for what I went through week after week with him. When he was a boy during the depression, a quarter might have been big shit, but now, I can't even buy the cheese crap out of the machine with a quarter. I'd rather get a "thank you" any day than that damn quarter. It's insulting—it's like I do it for that damn quarter? I do it because I'm nice, damnit! Not because I can't wait to get my grubby little peon hands all over that slimy quarter. Looking back, if I had smiled and been friendlier I could've gotten a much better reaction from most of those people. Being untrusting and defensive and plain pissed off in a lot of cases got me either no reaction or an unfriendly one.

Sometimes people were really cool, though. I'd help someone with an overheating problem and they'd be appreciative and give me a "big" thanks and maybe three or four bucks. Those were the moments that made humans seem, well, almost human.

Mike Pearson

One Step Beyond

Jeff, The Canyon, and Vehicles Al Diablo
"Stay Cat Strut" by Stray Cats

I wanted to get my friend Jeff to work at the station with me. Andre and Tony were good for a few laughs, but I didn't have anything in common with them. Eddie and Klaus were cool, but I wanted a friend my own age to work with me. Jeff was a surfing buddy of mine who lived in Santa Monica Canyon.

The people who lived in The Canyon were often laidback and artsy; a lot of them were hippies, nature-lovers or horse people. That was before prices went through the roof in the eighties and you had to be a millionaire to even think about living there.

Santa Monica Canyon divides Pacific Palisades and Santa Monica. It's woodsy, shady and rustic with little branching roads and lots of big eucalyptus trees. There is a creek at the bottom that empties into the ocean at the north side of the gas station's parking lot.

The canyon creek was like a mystical transportation system for us when we were younger. We'd hike up the dark fifteen-foot-tall rectangular pipe to a huge cement drainage ditch called Tony Alva's Secret Spot to go skateboarding. The spot was named after the legendary skateboarder who pioneered vertical riding in swimming pools in the seventies. It was about a five-mile walk from our junior high, Paul Revere, which was about five more miles up the canyon from the beach.

We'd ditch school and just skateboard straight down the tunnel to the beach. It went right through the Riviera Country Club. It wasn't covered in that section and we'd poke our heads up and scream when golfers would take their swing, making them choke.

The canyon was beautiful. A friend of mine lived on a property that looked like a tropical island. They bought the house of the guy who landscaped a lot of Disneyland. That was what their place was like. They had a creek running next to the house and there were strange tropical plants everywhere. When I was there I always expected to run into monkeys.

Jeff lived down the creek from them in a '50s modern house. I liked Jeff even though he hated people a lot and complained endlessly about having to put out effort toward girls and work and surfing (which was a lot like the way I was), but he jumped in and did all these things anyway (which was not like me), which made him an inspiration. He was a whiner and a consummate complainer in many ways, but he was also impulsive and had an ability to just go for it, whatever it was.

Jeff and I would surf almost every day out in front of the gas station during junior-high. We had such a blast out there. The water was full of neighborhood kids. The same fifty kids would be out there every day in front of lifeguard station 18. It was like an amusement park. The waves were often small, but really fun with good form. That was until there was this really bad storm at the end of the seventies that tore the beach apart. The sand bars that the waves broke off of had been flattened out. It was depressing to even go down there then because the whole beach was covered with little gray rocks instead of nice smooth sand and the waves crashed right on the shore. That storm had devastated the canyon and ruined many homes. I remember a car even got washed into the creek and the torrents carried it out to the ocean. This happened because the water level of the creek rose above the street by a foot or two. It was wild; practically everything that wasn't nailed down washed out to the sea. The bottom line for us, though, was that the waves were wrecked. They pounded right on shore for three years straight, and to this day the wave shape is still too walled. The long rides of yesterday were gone, so Jeff and I now had to drive to go surfing. I'd go over to his house early in the morning at about five when it was still dark.

"Hey, Jeff, wake up, you lazy ass. It's pumping out there. We're missing it."

"How do you know, Mike? It's dark. I'm sleepy, man."

Jeff's bed, just a mattress, lay on the floor. None of my friends had box springs except for me; I always felt different that way, not as cool.

"You can hear it!" I said. "Listen ... It's pumping!" And, sure enough, you could hear it. Jeff lived close to the ocean. A big, building, rumbling crashing sound, soft then louder, medium then louder, then really loud, like thunder.

"Jeff! Let's get out there!"

"Shut up, Mike, you're going to wake my mom and dad."

Jeff was cool. He was a good guy. I really wanted him to work at the station. It was spring and the beach was coming alive and I knew Klaus would need a couple more guys for summer. I had to get Jeff in there.

Klaus already knew Jeff, because his family had been customers for many years. Klaus knew Jeff's parents pretty well: his mom, Linda, was a spacey, artsy, sixties kind of mom; and his dad, Sheldon, a mellow psychiatrist.

Klaus also remembered Jeff's little brother, who died six years earlier at the age of ten, because of kidney failure (his kidneys were malformed from birth then finally gave out). I had never met Jeff's little brother, but it wasn't hard to understand why Linda was so protective of Jeff.

He was her first child and her last.

Jeff was so cynical and pessimistic. He challenged everything. He was a walking Mr. Devil's Advocate. I think his brother's death really affected him that way.

Jeff often explained things to me:

"Oh, Mike, that guy is so bad. You don't even know how fucked he is. That ... guy's ... such ... a dick."

And he always said things slowly while squinting, about Mr. Three Fingers, or whoever happened to be giving him a hard time.

He'd say, "Oh, Mike, you don't want to do that—you know that's not going to be any good."

It wasn't horrible the way Jeff complained. I thought it was kind of funny. He approached everything with a sense of doom but always ended up doing it anyway. He was always up to something.

Jeff got into weight lifting for a while.

Jeff made his own surfboards from scratch.

Jeff went to Fiji, got a girlfriend, was robbed by a lunatic, and got trapped on a weird island and they wouldn't let him off unless he paid major bucks; he didn't, and stayed awhile longer than expected.

Jeff worked as a used car salesman for scumbags.

Jeff went to Japan, excited as hell, to teach English and came back after a week. Hated it.

Jeff took about ten years of Jujitsu lessons so he could kick someone's ass if they needed to be taught a lesson. Usually, when Jeff was harassed by some jerk, he just looked at them like a raving lunatic with that bulging eyeball effect and then he would scream out at the top of his lungs in a terrifying way as he assumed a Bruce Lee position, and they would just take a step back and go:

"It's cool, man."

Jeff started working at the gas station in January of '82. Eddie and I got him all pumped up about cars. That's all we would talk about. Within a couple weeks, Jeff bit the bullet and purchased a worn-out 1967 Mustang off an old lady. He got really into fixing it. He replaced the majority of parts on that car, all with major Jeff-style frustration. Many hours and thousands of dollars later, the car was nearing completion. Then he slid out in the rain, careened into a curb, and bent his suspension into a pretzel, not only once, but twice, in two months. Jeff spent so much energy on that car, that by the time he got it in decent shape, he resented and hated it; he sold it for the same price he had paid for it (minus the million dollars he put in).

Mike Pearson

My first project car was "The Monster" ("The Monst," for short). I talked my parents into getting it for me in tenth grade. It cost $2,300. It was a brown 1973 Plymouth Road Runner. It had a motor home engine. I bought it off a local mechanic who had customized it. It got six miles-per-gallon, and had 450 horsepower and went from 0-60 in 5 seconds, without ever having to shift out of first! It wasn't very practical, unless you wanted to practically kill yourself and drain your bank account while paying for the gas to drive it.

I was only sixteen and here I was driving a car that could probably go 150 miles per hour. It would be suicidal to take it much above a hundred though, because it would start to shake so badly. But the car wasn't happy going slow either. The car was a beast and a pain in my ass. So I sold it to a crazy kid who took one week to destroy it. He smashed it into a wall.

Next, I bought Klaus's '64 Thunderbird, the pinnacle of all bad car experiences. The thing had been sitting there for over a decade at the station doing nothing. I finally convinced him to sell it to me. Before Klaus, it belonged to a German doctor who had yanked my tonsils when I was young. The car, as Klaus said:

"Is such a piece of shit, Michael, you don't want it."

"Yes, I do—I need it."

Here I was drooling over this faded beige machine.

Klaus sold it to me for five hundred bucks.

It was a classic.

I was now the proud owner of a classic piece of junk. It had a slide-over steering wheel, which made it easier to get in the car, and a speedometer that looked like mercury traveling sideways in a thermometer.

I jumped inside to start it up, turned the key, and it fired up instantly. It sounded like utter and complete shit, but nothing "a little elbow grease couldn't take care of." It was staggering and choking, barely running, and made loud popping noises through its perforated rusted-out muffler.

It ran for about one minute before bursting into flames. While it ran for that minute, gas was sputtering out of the old rotted gas line and it spurted onto the engine. Then the whole engine went up in flames. The flames began to roar as a major disaster unfolded before me. I panicked. This was a gas station, a place with A LOT of gas! I grabbed the fire extinguisher and tried putting out the flames, but Klaus took it away from me and rapidly and skillfully extinguished it. Then he became really angry and screamed:

"Goddamn it, Michael! Why did you have to use the fucking fire extinguisher? You know you don't use that! Now I have to get the thing recharged!"

I stood there in utter amazement.

"What?" I said. "The heap I just bought from you five seconds ago, burst into flames, destroying the whole engine compartment and you're complaining to me about a fire extinguisher? Now I own this crispy, burnt piece of Thunderbird shit and you're complaining to me about your fire extinguisher?"

I could understand, though. Klaus wasn't mad about the fire extinguisher. He was mad because the car burst into flames.

Klaus told me that he'd help me fix the car, and he did. But it was up to me to replace every wire, tube, hose and basically anything that wasn't metal. And it took me 10,000 hours. Klaus helped me on the hard stuff, like the power brake unit. He told me he never wanted to sell it to me in the first place, because, in his words, he'd "end up married to the piece of shit."

The poorly rebuilt power-brake unit broke down within a week and needed to be replaced again. I didn't have the heart to ask Klaus to help me again. I didn't even tell him what happened. I was so frustrated. I had just about got up the nerve to roll it off the cliff by my house when a painter who my mom had over one day decided he wanted it, for 500 bucks.

The thing was chugging and farting, barely idling, but he bought it. The poor guy didn't even make it up to his house in Topanga Canyon. Before I knew it, he called up, whining and moaning, and my dad got on the phone and told him:

"You bought it in 'as-is' condition. Good-bye."

I felt bad for the guy, but it was gone, and that was the most important thing.

Over the next few weeks I learned more and more about cars, and whenever somebody came into the station with a problem, I would run to get my hands on their car first, before Eddie or Jeff. Even if I had never done the type of repair before, there always had to be a first time.

However, the motorist didn't have to know that and never did.

Sometimes I'd get stuck and start asking Eddie quietly about why that bolt broke off in the engine and if it mattered.

"Mechanics" often resort to 'Mickey Mousing' it.

Which means:

When it's too hard to do the job right (or do it at all for that matter), you just have to do it wrong or anyway possible. And don't think this practice is exclusive to gas stations and crummy little shops. Yes, even "The Dealer" is involved in this conspiracy.

Eddie was the Mickey-Mouse Job Master. One day Eddie was fighting for so long trying to get this goddamn fuel pump on. What he had to do was get this small-lever, which was located just inside the engine, to stay up while he slipped the fuel pump in, which also had a lever on it that was in the way.

I stood there, eating Cheetos, watching him try time and time again with the pump. The little lever kept falling down in the way. Then, finally, he wiped his brow, took a breath and asked me for a Cheeto.

"Here, let me have one of those."

I handed him a Cheeto expecting him to pop it into his mouth but, instead, he took it and wedged it into the engine to hold that goddamn lever up. It worked. It was holding the lever in place.

He slipped on the pump, screwed on the two bolts, then started that sucker up, and I imagined that Cheeto being blown into a million pieces ... into the oil ... little orange fragments circulating all around in that engine.

It wouldn't really hurt anything, it was just a Cheeto, but that was pretty ridiculous.

And the owner probably had him do an oil change, too, right before that. To Eddie, what counted was that it worked to get that pump on. After he started the engine I put on a serious face and asked him,

"Eddie, but what about the Cheeto?"

And he looked at me dead serious and said:

"Sometimes, Mike-man, you just gotta put the fuckin' Cheeto in there."

At this point it was June and I'd be not graduating from high school in a couple weeks. I'd get a diploma, but I wouldn't go to the ceremony. I didn't feel a part of Venice, so I said forget it. I also blew off the prom. With whom would I go even if I wanted to? Tony? Andre? Klaus? I had no girls in my life, but I sure thought about girls a lot. I was just too shy to go out and meet them and try something. Unconsciously, I figured I'd make due with cars and motorcycles for a while.

The day after I finished high school I went on a motorcycle ride in the Malibu hills with my old friend Steve. I hadn't seen Steve much since he became obsessed with his motorcycle. I had a fast street bike too, but I didn't ride it often. I had had a few close encounters with death and was freaked out about the bike. It was a Yamaha Seca 550 and it went 0-60 in 4.1 seconds. It spent most of its time sitting in my garage.

Steve, on the other hand, rode every day and had a lot of experience. He would take long trips averaging 100 miles a day, and ride incredibly fast the whole way. His family life was chaotic and disturbing, and both parents were alcoholics. He was an angry kid who had a definite death wish. Flying like a bat out of hell on a motorcycle, or perhaps dead, was better than being stuck at home in the growing negativity and darkness of a bad family life.

I was terrified trying to keep up with him. He always rode way out ahead of me and although I tried, he was impossible to catch. Honestly, he rarely went slower than seventy or eighty miles an hour, unless he was going through a tight turn, where the rule of thumb was double the speed limit. Several times the LAPD tried to catch him, succeeding only once because they chased him with a helicopter. Every other time he out ran them. Every time I rode with him I almost crashed. On one particular Death Wish Steve ride, I found myself on a straight country road between San Diego and Blythe, Arizona, with a slow moving farm truck, heading toward me. The trucker pulled an incredibly slow-motion left in front of my bike. I was only able to brake from a hundred to about eighty. The whole thing came down to: if this lazy-ass was going to make the turn super fucking slow, which meant that I would splatter into the side, or just really fucking slow, which meant I'd go blasting past just barely missing his back bumper. The latter was the case, obviously.

I had this plan to go for another ride with Steve. It had been a while, and my fear had subsided some. I felt kind of guilty; I hadn't done anything with him in months. He said he was beginning to slow down on the bike, that he'd been worried lately himself.

We rode up Old Topanga Road into the Malibu hills. We turned on to Mulholland Drive and went north along the top of the mountain between the ocean and the valley. As we headed through Topanga a couple different hippie-types screamed at us as we passed, "Slow Down!" because, even though we thought we were going "slow" (at fifty), it was still too fucking fast for a quiet country road. We sailed past the famous Rock Shop, where hundreds of bikers hang out and race each other on weekends. We kept going up the mountain road and took in a view of the ocean at the top, and then we headed back down the way we came. We maneuvered around a skinny winding road that hugged the side of the mountain. Steve was in front of me going fifty around a blind curve when an oblivious driver in a station wagon did a u-turn directly in front of him. The driver was facing the blind curve as we came around it. He made his turn about twelve feet right in front of Steve.

I watched Steve bounce off the passenger door in slow motion. He and the motorcycle elevated like a balloon above the top of the wagon, about six feet in the air, and it all came down in a mangled heap. I rode right by, not realizing that it was Steve who was hit. I was in denial. "It couldn't be possible, it couldn't be him."

.

One Step Beyond

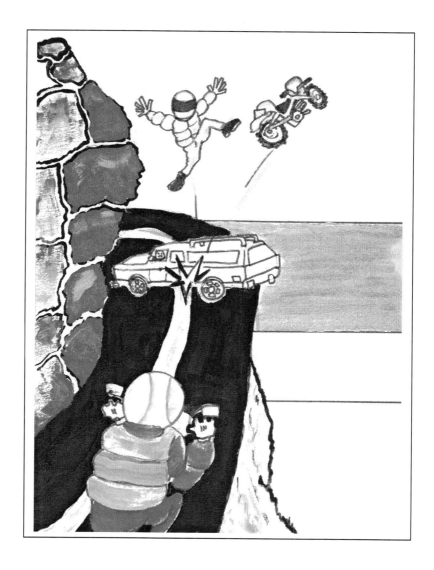

A little further down the road it started to seep in and I slowed down and turned around. I felt dazed and I was dizzy with hot flashes. I got off my motorcycle and my legs were wobbling as I stood over my friend's broken, rag doll body. His joints were bent up in wrong directions. It was almost impossible to believe it was true. This was my friend. Then suddenly I realized what had happened and I was enraged. I yelled at the man who was still sitting in the car.

"Look what you did to my friend! You fucking idiot!"

He and his wife were dazed, just sitting in the car, too spineless and taken aback to get out and see if they could help. They just sat there looking dumbfounded, like "What do we do now, honey." I yelled at them some more.

They just sat there speechless.

The helicopter flew in and landed, stirring up a cloud of dust next to us. The paramedics cut off most of Steve's clothes and straightened out his limbs the best they could as he moaned and screamed and foamed at the mouth. Then they moved him onto a stretcher and flew away. I went to the pay phone and called his mom. The poor guy spent the next two months in the hospital.

He had a pretty serious head injury (even though he had been wearing a helmet); he had to have his brain drained because pressure was building in his skull due to fluid. He also had two broken legs, a broken wrist, four broken ribs and major bruising. He was extremely lucky though. They said it was a miracle. After a lot of physical therapy and hospitalization, he recovered completely. It took about a year total. That was the world's biggest wake-up call for that kid, and for me, too. I had to become a more careful person because I didn't want to die young.

I was so terrified by the whole experience that I couldn't actually believe it happened.

The world seemed a threatening place to me; a place where friends drop you, friends bust you, people in cars run you over and don't apologize.

I decided to get rid of the motorcycle immediately. I rang up a guy whom we called Hag.

"Hey, Hag, you want my 550? I'm done."

"Yeah, man, it's a cool bike, but the Suzuki..."

I traded it to him for a '66 Mustang GT Fastback plus a thousand bucks.

Hag had the bike now, thank God, and I had his messed-up, black, faded '66 GT Mustang Fastback, which needed a ton of work but could be awesome.

Just as I figured, Hag drove that motorcycle like a complete lunatic for about a week until he went to a Hancock Park party and it got ripped off, which was lucky for him. The motorcycle getting ripped off was the best thing that could've happened to Hag. He would've killed himself for sure on it.

The next day, back at the gas station, I told everybody what had happened and they just got in line quickly to share their accident stories. "Oh, that's nothing—check this one out!"

Stuff doesn't sink in to a lot of guys. They shrug shit off like it's no big deal. So I tried to shrug it off. Who knew how traumatized I was? I didn't know. The guys at the gas station reacted the same to everything that happened, whether it's your friend getting minced in a motorcycle accident or a water pump that's stuck. They were all so desensitized and disassociated.

It would be right to be concerned that our desensitization might eventually be our downfall, turning us more and more brittle until someday we just fracture, crack and crumble.

Anyway, I tried to get Eddie to stop joking around for long enough so I could talk to him about more serious matters.

Engine rebuilding. I was trying to put the accident out of my head. There was no time for post-traumatic stress disorder when a Mustang needed rebuilding. I threw myself into fixing the car: a slight of hand, a magic trick. What accident? Look over here. Rebuild the car; you can do that. You can't rebuild your friend, so leave that to the doctors, but you can fix this Mustang.

The Mustang didn't even run. It was a true wreck. It was dented all over it. It had five different types of paint. Nothing worked properly. Its steering and suspension were completely shot. My mom and the neighborhood rent-a-cop helped push it up our steep driveway. The car wobbled into my garage on its hobbled, knock-kneed suspension.

I opened the hood and stared at the engine. I was now ready to perform my first engine overhaul. I didn't have an engine hoist, though, which you need to get the engine out, and I didn't really want to go rent one, because, shit, I didn't know how to take the engine out of a car! So I figured that maybe the bottom-end of the engine wasn't in such bad condition after all. I could probably get away with just an upper-end valve-job.

One Step Beyond

I started the project one night with a house lamp balanced on the fender to see by. I took my ratchet and put it onto one of the bolts on the water-pump. This was the first step: to take the water-pump off. I slowly began twisting the bolt, slowly, slowly—

Clunk!

It broke off in my ratchet.

That's okay. That only meant that I had to go on the first of about eight hundred thousand trips to the auto-parts store to buy tools. I had to get something that might possibly enable me to get that fucking bolt out!

In a situation like this, you basically drill a hole in the center of the broken off bolt, then you insert a screw—that you tighten in counter-clockwise—and then you keep twisting and twisting and, finally, the bolt unscrews.

That's in theory, but what really happens, is the counter-clockwise screw-thing breaks off in the broken-off bolt. And then what do you do? Perform microsurgery and insert another screw thing? No. You have to go get a big ass drill bit, and get really pissed off and drill the whole fucking bolt out, if you can. The metal's so hard, though, it slips around. To do that, you have to take the whole engine out and get the hole rethreaded.

No fucking way! Take the engine out?

So, I just said to heck with it and left that broken off thing in there and politely asked the other five remaining bolts to be nice and hold it tight enough so it wouldn't leak. To my amazement, it obeyed with the help of about a pint of gasket sealer.

The next day, I went to work and I saw Eddie. He was fixing a car in the lube bay. I asked him what he thought about me doing a valve job on the Mustang without taking the bottom-end out to be machined. (The bottom-end is the pistons and cylinders and big stuff that often doesn't get as damaged because it's bigger and tougher.)

Eddie would always blab on and on as if he knew just what the hell he was talking about. But how much he knew, I was doubtful.

I figured he had to know at least more than I did. That's why I asked him. Eddie's response to my question went like this:

"Mike, man, you take out those heads and you send 'em out, and you get 'em all perfect and tight and sealing off all the air, all perfect and shit, with no leaks and the thing is just sealing away, like running all perfect and sano up at the top-end ... And you leave the bottom-end alone!—And it's all loose and fucked up and it starts freaking out ... and then it starts shooting, spitting, air past those cylinders ... which are so loose anyway from all those hundreds and thousands of miles of wear! ... And the top end—those valves—are sealing off like all perfecto—tight and shit—and the air and the oil and the water—from the water-jackets being so fucked up!—is just rushing past the sides of those cylinders—and the whole thing is just blowing oil past those pistons ... And it's all shaking and fucked up—And then the whole thing is just going to take a big shit and die right there!"

"Gee, Eddie, thanks for your opinion."

So, maybe it's a bad idea?

Oh well, I'll just go ahead and do it anyway. And the thing was, it turned out fine. I loved proving to nervous, anxious people (myself included) that things can be okay.

That wasn't to say that Mustang wasn't a major pain in my ass.

Mike Pearson

Girl Disturbed
"I Ran" by Flock Of Seagulls

The Mustang was frustrating and took a lot of work, but it kept me busy and distracted for a while. I felt so lonely, though. I was tired of being single, alone, without a girlfriend. It seemed I had always been on my own. I had never had a serious girlfriend. I was sick of hanging out with just guys, insensitive, tough, macho guys. I needed some warmth, some understanding, and a little nurturing. I didn't know how to provide that for myself. I wanted a girlfriend to do it for me. Then, maybe I'd be happy. Cars, guy friends, and my own weak self-nurturing skills weren't filling the emptiness.

There was one girl I knew I was attracted to, my friend Robbie's little sister, Amy. I thought I'd try for her. I met her one night after getting off work from the station. Robbie lived one block from the gas station in the canyon. I met her while playing music at Robbie's house with my friends. We were in Robbie's room playing cover songs. I played bass. Robbie was on guitar, my friend Alex was on guitar, and another friend, Boney, was on guitar. Everyone played guitar and they all sang. We would each take turns rotating in and playing crappy drums. We all had cheap, bad equipment and our amplifiers were little. Steve was there, too, just hanging out.

We played "Submission" by the Sex Pistols, which sounded real wimpy and submissive, and that was a shame, because they were one of my favorite groups, and they didn't deserve to have their song played so pathetically by geeks. But "Submission" was one of those easy three chord songs and we could play it, so that was that. My friends traded off duties singing away in fake Johnny Rotten English accents when I caught my first glimpse of Robbie's little sister.

I saw her pass by the open door to Robbie's room. She peeked in, smiled, and waved at us and kept going right on by with a confident bob in her walk. She was fifteen years old, beautiful, slim, with a fantastic smile, blonde hair, and what seemed like a dynamic charge of energy.

I watched her disappear around the corner. Then I looked around at my friends. I stopped playing.

"Holy! What the?" I didn't know what word to use next.

"Hey ... Hey," Alex said, trying to knock some sense into me. "Mike, that's Robbie's little sister. She's in ninth grade!"

Robbie glared at me.

"I can respect that ... not really. But did you see that!"

"Dude, she's Brand Nubian," my friend Boney said reasonably.

"I can respect that, not really," I repeated.

"Mike, man..." and Jeff was about to come down on me. Then he sighed. "She is hot, huh?"

"Okay, start the song already," Robbie commanded. Robbie counted: "1, 2, 3, 4."

We started playing. It sounded like crap. Everyone at the same time figured out that I was a full step off in the wrong key,

"Mike," Robbie yelped angrily. "Get it together!"

Robbie was pissed. He was protective of Amy, but, beyond that, he was jealous. His sister was always stealing attention from him, first with his parents, now with us. He knew now that she was always going to be the number one distraction when it came to everyone.

"Your sister's so cute, though," I pointed out.

"Ninth grade, Mike? Ninth grade!" he reiterated.

I screamed in my head:

"You think my hormones know what fucking grade she's in? They don't know! They don't care!" That's what I wanted to yell. But Robbie was a nice guy. I liked him, but something was going on with him. He had a really happy sweet attitude, but he seemed to have some anger buried, because every now and then he'd completely blow his top. He'd just go crazy. His family had the perfect outward appearance. Fantastic looking parents, good manners, really friendly…but who knew what lurked beneath the facade of Mr. and Mrs. Perfect USA. I think they were one of those families where no one is allowed to express anything but "happy, happy, grateful, and grateful" all the time.

They looked kind of like the Osmond's. And Robbie looked just like Donny Osmond. He had big, thick, brown hair that swirled all around his head. He was a cute guy, but he wasn't really ready for girls yet. He shied away from them. He was happier playing guitar with the guys and listening to the Stray Cats.

Alex didn't seem like he could deal much with girls, either, and Jeff was definitely nervous about them. Hell, we were all anxious about girls. Maybe that was a part of why we were friends: we were on a similar level developmentally. Freaked out.

I was nervous about girls but compelled to try anyway. I was ready to go over to Robbie's house constantly and attempt to woo his sister. I figured she'd take a lot of work. I didn't know that that was the wrong attitude! The right attitude was: this will be no problem, easy.

For me: it wasn't easy. Why? Because I didn't know what the hell I was doing! I had gone out with a few girls here and there. I had made out with girls off and on since 4th grade. Actually I had more experiences back in elementary than in either junior high or high school.

Elementary School? My elementary was full of perverts, probably because we were products of perpetually nude and the super inappropriate sexually revolutionary '70s with NO boundaries. Youngsters were always pairing up and going into the ball-box for make-out sessions. (The ball-box was the room where they handed out the balls at recess.) A kid who was the attendant would wave us past after checking that the coast was clear.

We'd make out and report to our peers what base we made it to. Second or third base was common. A few kids in the school were advanced. One sixth-grade couple went all the way in the Goodwill box out in front of the Safeway market. In fourth grade, I watched two of my nine-year-old neighbors have sex standing up. They pulled down their pants, and the boy said, "Look what we do!" I was like what the hell?

They didn't even know what it was called. They thought they invented it. I did too. I felt they were pretty insane.

So far my first and only experience "doing it" was back in tenth grade. I had always dreamed of having a girlfriend with a good personality who was pretty. I was so passive and sensitive to rejection that I never made assertive moves on girls. So I was left with aggressive girls who would pursue me.

I got Sue Berg.

I talked to Sue on the phone every night during tenth grade. We'd talk sometimes for six hours straight. We sure had a lot to say to each other. Sometimes we'd talk all through the night till it was morning. My ears would get really sore from the phone. I liked her a lot as a friend. She was interesting and had a lot on her mind. She wanted to be more than friends though. She had a big crush on me. She was always pushing me to do things in real life, in person, and not just on the phone. I kept it to phone buddies. We talked for months (I wasn't conscious of how much she really liked me), and I unknowingly tortured her by telling her about how much I liked these other girls. I was so naïve. I thought, she's my good friend: Hmm, maybe she'll put in a good word for me or give me some good advice. The reality didn't sink in to my thick skull for a long time. I guess I didn't want it to.

It never worked out with the other girls I liked, I would wait so long before making a move that things became uncomfortable, strange and ultimately, boring. They knew I was a big wuss. I was too insecure and timid. But I kept talking to Sue on the phone until it escalated to phone sex. We started saying horny, sexy things to each other, and it finally got to the point where I started describing in detail what I was going to do to her. Whenever I saw her in person at school, I was always disturbed by how much I wasn't attracted to her. She had a great body, but I just wasn't attracted to her face. I was frustrated with myself. I wished I were more attracted to her. For a long time I used the old (as girls often say about guys they don't like enough):

"I really value our friendship too much to risk it."

She insisted on how great it would be if we had sex, how incredibly wonderful it would be, how damn awesome it would be!

So, I figured, it couldn't be that bad.

Finally, after so much pursuit on her part, I said, "What the fuck? I'm going for it."

A year earlier my mom had given me the keys to my grandma's condo in case I wanted to bring a girl there. It was vacant because Gram only stayed there about two days a year; she hated being alone (she had no friends) and liked living with us. The condo sat there empty, year round. My mom handed me the keys along with an embarrassing speech.

"This is for you if you ever want to bring a girl up there, but use condoms. Blah, blah, blah."

"Oh, my God, Mom! SHUT UP!" I took the keys from her.

I told Sue we could go there. So, there we were one Friday night. Sitting on the couch. This is a foreign environment, no music, Grandma furniture, Grandma everything. It has a gold '60s vibe, with cottage cheese ceiling, crusty, and outdated. Everything was perfectly in place. What a scene!

I fumbled around with her, petting, kissing, uncomfortably on the couch for about thirty minutes. She seemed to be in the moment, enjoying it, but I was really nervous and ambivalent and thinking too much. Then she moaned, "Let's go to the bedroom."

"Oh, no," I said. "We can't mess up the bed." Then I thought of more inane reasons how to get out of it.

"My grandma will find out. She'll shit. We can't fuck this place up."

But Sue smiled at me eagerly.

"Don't worry about it. We'll make the bed after."

Then I followed her into the room and I looked at the bed. It was perfectly made.

"We'll never be able to make it as good as it is now," I whined. But she cut me off, smiled happily, and said,

"It'll be okay."

So we got into the bed.

We started making out heavily. We took each other's clothes off. We were naked. I was ready, but extremely nervous. I tried to get it in. But there wasn't enough lubrication. She wasn't that comfortable either, though she was acting like she was.

She said was going to look for something in the bathroom that would lubricate. She got up and went in there. She was fumbling around in the bathroom for a few minutes. Then she brought back a jar of Vaseline. I had a feeling that

that wasn't the right stuff. Well, we used it and it didn't make things easier, just more disturbing and difficult actually. Finally, we got it going, but what a battle.

Then, after about ten minutes, we were done and I wanted to scream: "Can we go now!" but didn't have the nerve.

And then, as we were making the bed, I noticed, to my horror, the aftermath. A giant wet spot on the sheet.

"Is that going to stain?" I screamed.

Just kidding. I didn't say that.

So I tried to make the bed properly. I was hoping that my grandma wouldn't find "the spot."

The experience freaked me out. Sue said it was wonderful, but I thought, If that's wonderful, I wonder what bogus is like? After that, surprisingly, I didn't want to go out with her and be her boyfriend. I avoided her. Within a day or two she was enraged at me.

"I was used!" she said to friends and family. "What an asshole!"

She was used? I thought. What about me? I felt like a disembodied dildo for Chrissakes.

I guess she thought that if we had sex that would be the clincher and I'd be committed and become her boyfriend. That would seal the deal. I'd become enlightened through the sexual experience and then I'd bond with her.

She didn't understand that a young guy like me could do it without ending up feeling closer. Afterward, I felt even less.

Many people have said, "Sex will wreck the friendship." In this case they were right.

I went into the local market a few days later and saw her sister working in the bakery section. To my naïve surprise, she approached me, pissed as hell and chewed me out. She told me what an asshole I was and how I took advantage of her sister. I was disturbed. I felt like a bad guy. Was I a bad guy? Did I fuck her over?

Now, at 17, I thought little Amy might just be the answer for my girlfriend blues. I wouldn't have to set limits with her; she wasn't the kind to intrude on me and get in my business. There was no way I was going to get her! My thinking was, younger girl, someone to take it easy with, no pressure, just cruising, have some fun. She was really cute too.

I was back at Robbie's playing the Clash's "Should I Stay Or Should I Go" with the guys. Then we rocked some Stray Cats. Their album was kind of small still, and we felt cool, like we were underground. As I played the songs all I could think about was Amy. She was so cute.

I couldn't believe my friends weren't interested in her. She went ignored.

I suppose she was "too young" that's what they said, and she was Robbie's sister. Whatever the reason, she was not to be considered. I had a problem; I could just not stop thinking about her.

At night, when the other guys had gone home, I would end up staying, which meant talking to Amy for hours under the pretense of watching TV. She would tell me about the guys she liked, and this and that, and that and this, and the other thing. I listened, and I gave advice.

And—

I was so stupid! I had already blown it! She just didn't like me.

Mr. Nice Guy. I was doomed. But I didn't know it and kept trying anyway.

God, I should have given up. Sometimes that's the best idea. Just give up. I wasn't familiar with that age-old piece of advice: If at first you don't succeed, quit! Move on!

I thought she would be mine if I were just Mr. Nice Boy Listener, The Nicest Guy. (A recipe for disaster!) Eventually she'd come around and realize, "I love this guy."

I was in Fantasyland.

Amy liked bad boy "scammers," models, surfed-out, gyrated dudes who were just into "boning down on chicks." Anyway, I hung in there like a crash-test dummy, hearing about all her dramas, thinking that someday she would drop the irrational approach, become rational, and go for me. Not on her life.

By mid-summer she had had soap opera style relationships with most of the stud guys on the beach. Her fantasies were realized as I stood by as her eunuch advisor.

That was the summer of Flock of Seagulls' "I Ran (So Far Away)."

I wish I had run so far away from her.

And Missing Persons' "What are Words for?"

Tell her I'm not going to take this blue ball shit any longer!

One Step Beyond

Even Steve Miller had a new-wave song, "Abracadabra" (I wanna reach out and grab ya!).

I wanted to reach out and grab her! But no!

My friend Alex made me so frustrated. I was so jealous of him. Many girls were attracted to him, and it was no surprise when Amy told me she had a crush on him. He was dark and handsome and had some cool Marlon Brando mannerisms. He liked Marlon Brando and James Dean, and their movies rubbed off on him. He might have even studied them. He also had cool Clint Eastwood squints and so forth in his repertoire. He wasn't that motivated to get involved with girls, though. Sure he liked to find out about those who liked him, but the knowledge of this seemed to be good enough for him. He didn't really want to deal with girls, too many variables, and too many worries.

So he was a challenge to girls, disinterested, not needing their drama, and this made him even more desirable. He wasn't into Amy. He said she was too self-involved, "too young." And that's probably what I liked about her. Life seemed to revolve around her; she was intense, passionate. He didn't want to deal with that. I did.

Amy talked to me all about him, and pathetically I listened and provided counsel. I had been trained all too well by mom throughout my childhood to listen with helpless and endless frustration with no understanding of its effect on my soul.

Amy asked me repeatedly, "Why doesn't Alex like me?" She couldn't understand it because all guys were attracted to her. Pretty much any dude who saw her wanted her (at least for a scam), except Alex. Within a month, I had become frustrated with this crap, but apparently not frustrated enough, 'cause I was still hanging in there, listening patiently, waiting for her to come around, become sensible and go for me, the nice guy who was there for her.

I knew I had to find a way to get her out of my head, and out of my life. The pointlessness of it was now beyond obvious. The frustration would have to get worse though before I would finally let go. I was just too much of a champion at sucking on crumbs. I was so familiar with this dynamic that I couldn't get irritated enough to bail. It would take a couple months more.

One Step Beyond

Mike Pearson

Summer
Lords Of Oil
"Cars" by Gary Numan

Summer was here. Alex got a job at the gas station. He was very into it from the minute he started. From all his enthusiasm I became more inspired too. We didn't need to work seventy hours a week, and I don't really know why we did. It was just fun, I suppose. Sometimes you just get into something, without thinking about it much, and you just figure that it's good. Every day through June, Alex and I arrived at either eight or ten in the morning and stayed until ten at night. One week I worked eighty hours and Alex hit the record another week at 84. Clearly we were glad to be out of our depressing home environments.

Another reason we pushed the limit on hours was because for every hour over forty we would get time-and-a-half, which meant we would get $5.25 instead of the usual measly $3.50. That would enable us to pull in about $225 a week, which seemed like a lot at the time—at least compared to the usual 90 bucks for thirty hours.

Soon enough, Klaus was typing our paychecks and it sank in.

He screamed out:

"Mike and Alex!"

We walked around the corner to his little office.

"What the fuck! Goddamn you work fucking eighty hours in one week! What are you trying to do, ruin me?"

"Sorry, Klaus," I said.

Alex explained, "We just lost track of how much we worked."

Klaus knew how much we were working, because he was there with us every hour of every day. How could he miss us? He must have enjoyed our company, because he never told us to go home. And we told him straight-out that overtime was the only way we could make any money there because $3.50 sucked so badly.

Klaus replied: "Fuck you ...you ahsoles don't need the money. You can get it from your fucking dads. You can buy this fucking place from me if you want. You rich cocksuckers."

We took this only as Klaus's way of being friendly. We were not starving. True. Klaus himself wasn't poor. He would like us to think that, though. The simple truth was that the station made a bundle.

This was no average gas station. This was a major landmark: one of the first gas stations at the end of the whole Interstate freeway system (the 10), the freeway that goes right across the whole United States from east to west. You can start driving in New York, a week or two later arrive in California, at the beach, and the first person you might meet could be Klaus. You may never want to come to California again.

One Step Beyond

It was the perfect location, especially in the summer when everyone goes to the beach.

Alex and I recruited practically every one of our friends to work there at this point. We took the place over. Andre was already gone, fired for too much messing around. Tony would quit within a week; he had found a higher paying job.

The crew now consisted of me, Jeff, Alex, Robbie, Boz "The Dirty White Boy," and Jimmy. Jimmy had just started and quickly became a father figure to all of us. We were so lucky to have Jimmy there with us. He was about fifty, originally from Mexico. Jimmy was such a nice, loving man and only looking back now do I realize how much he cared about us. Diego was his nickname and Diego drank a lot of coffee out of small, white, Styrofoam cups.

Eddie would yell for Diego to help him with repairs, "Hey, Diego! Could you give me a hand with this brake shoe? It's a bitch. Fucker won't come off."

"Okay, Edder, hold on, my boy," Jimmy said as he drank the final sip from his Styrofoam cup. Jimmy slowly walked over. He just looked at the brake shoe for a moment. It was as if he was trying to get it to relax or something. Then he just took it off like it was never attached in the first place. Then he'd shrug and say, "Fucking, Edder, chinga tu madre."

"Hey," Eddie said, "How the..." with a look of amazement, like he'd just seen a magic trick. Eddie was always baffled by how talented Jimmy was with cars.

Jimmy seemed to enjoy working at the station with all of us. Sometimes he seemed a little depressed. No matter his mood, he was always kind to people. Jimmy had a big family with adult children. He showed us pictures of them and they would come by and visit and sometimes pick him up at closing time. They were nice. Jimmy drove a faded old American van.

I was surprised at how patient and helpful Jimmy was. He might have just been raised that way. I was used to my dad as a role model; he grew up "privileged," yet neglected, and he seemed impatient and disinterested in most people. He was an old-school Hollywood agent and I guess people expected him to yell at them with final offers and so forth. That was his generation's thing: hardboiled. I was happy Jimmy was around and in my life. He helped me more than I knew at the time. I liked how he was tolerant and patient and kind and didn't seem to let himself get too bothered by things. I think he understood that people were insane but he wasn't going to let them drive him nuts. He took situations in stride.

I loved the way Jimmy talked to us too.

He would say, "Yes, my boy."

He'd always call us, "My boy."

He'd say, "My boy, it's the fucking carburetor." but, with his accent, it came out like this:

"My boy is tee fuck-ing-car-bor-ray-tor."

And when he said it was tee fuck-ing-car-bor-ray-tor, it would always be tee fuck-ing-car-bor-ray-tor.

Or he would say: "Ees they fuck-ing fuel-pump."

"Eesapieceaschit" would be one word.

He'd always add too many verbs; for instance: "My boy, you must to go to go to do to do it yourself. You can do it. Yes, you can, my boy, you can."

He was so encouraging. I loved that. I needed that. The boys would always have faith that we could go to do to do it ourselves, because Jimmy told us we could. He was the best. I loved him.

Jimmy and I spent a lot of the slow time at the station sitting on the tailgate of Klaus's blue '58 Ford Ranchero. The Ranchero sat permanently in the furthest section of the lube-bay. When sitting there, staring at the ocean, it was all the way to the left.

Whenever someone pulled up while we were sitting there, our attitude was:

"Let's get rid of them, the faster the better."

One of us got the windows, another did the gas, a third person wrote up the credit card slip, the gas clicked off, they signed the card, and they were out of there.

And we were back on the tailgate.

My friends and I didn't socialize with customers much. That was sure Eddie's thing, though. Eddie would talk to all of them for hours straight if they let him. Not us, we wanted them out of there.

Eddie would listen to their horror stories about The Dealer From Hell. Then he would always have a little something to say about that. He'd take a look under their hoods and come out with it plain and simple:

"Linda, you got yourself a little valve gasket leak. If you bring it down in the morning, I'll put it up on the lift, unscrew a couple bolts, get some gasket sealer, paint it on there—smear it around a little—and put on a new gasket for you, as simple as that. Perfect. No problem.

"You're on the road again, and you can make it over to your doctor's appointment, and you can make it to work and visit your sweetheart, and everything is just bitchin'."

"—On the other hand, if you take it to the dealer, they're going to take the whole engine apart. They're gonna start fucking around with everything, they're going to say you need a new water-jacket spring, a heater propulsion unit, a piston valve, and then, they're gonna start replacing your cylinder heads! And they're going to take apart your whole exhaust system! And they're going to sell you three new mufflers—and then they're going to charge you about twenty million dollars!

"Since they put it back together all wrong, you're going to be on the road, on your way to the dentist, and the whole engine's going to blow up right there! It's just going to take a big shit right there on the 405 freeway!"

"You're going to have to call Triple A and miss your dentist appointment and since you've got gingivitis, your teeth are going to fall out right there on the highway, and you can't make it to work, so your boss fires your ass. No more job. And you finally get home three days later and your sweetheart sees you and you have no teeth left, and he says, "Where the fuck have you been?" and he's already got a new girlfriend lined up, 'cause the whole thing took so long. Then, he dumps you right there, and it's all over and you're totally fucked.

"So, Linda, I'm telling you, save yourself the hassle and bring it down in the morning and I'll fix it for you. No problem."

"Well, gee, Eddie, if you put it that way."

One Step Beyond

That's how Eddie was.

Robbie and Boz were the new guys. Another kid we knew had been hired but he ended up taking Klaus personally, so he quit after a week.

Both Robbie and Boz didn't know anything about cars before coming to the station, but that didn't stop them from pretending that they did. They jumped right into repairs. Whenever someone came in and needed a repair, there was no way they were going to turn it down and let more experienced people take care of it. They wanted to do it and they were on a mission.

Boz's nickname was "The Dirty White Boy," because he was translucently pasty and greasy and shiny. He was a good-natured guy, but annoyingly ambitious.

Robbie and Boz made a lot of mistakes in their first weeks.

Some examples:

Robbie put oil into the transmission, instead of the engine. Victim flipped out. Victim reported error. Klaus had to put the car up on the rack and drain it.

Boz found a "victim" for a tire repair and got very excited. This was his first chance to do tire repair because Alex, Jeff and I were faster spotting breakdowns and repair vehicles, and we usually got there first.

Boz got the air gun and attached it to the air hose. He put the air gun onto the lug nuts and started blasting away. There he went, one at a time. Only he was tightening them, instead of loosening them. He broke them off, one after the other, three in a row:

Whirr ... Ka-Plunk!

Whirr ... Ka-Plunk!

Whirr ... Ka-Plunk!

Then there were the situations that looked like mistakes but weren't, and the customers would go crazy just the same.

Robbie poured the oil in somebody's PCV-valve-socket on the valve cover of the engine (it goes into the engine just fine that way). The customer was standing there watching, and he lost his mind because the obvious place to put it in was in the spot marked "Oil". The man thought that Robbie had just destroyed his whole engine.

He screamed at Robbie:

"You stupid little shit ... What the fuck!" while pointing at the oil cap, "OIL."

Eddie heard the commotion and came casually strolling over.

Eddie put his arm condescendingly around the guy's shoulder, and said, "Hey, buddy ... just relax."

Eddie was more calm and casual than you've ever seen anybody in your life.

"Buddy...relaaax..." Eddie said, soothingly, as he raised his palms to the sky. "The fucking oil is all going into the same place anyway."

And the guy started to relax a little, easing up, but he was still way tense.

"You can put the oil in there," Eddie said, and he pointed to some valve or plug. And the man's shoulders lower a bit and he begins to breathe a little.

"You can put the oil in there," Eddie said, as he pointed to another location. "You can even put it in there. It doesn't matter. It's all going to the same place."

And Eddie started smiling, and the guy started smiling, and Eddie was thinking:

"Yeah, right—get the fuck out of here!"

Robbie and Boz were the most capitalistic of our group by far. They would have competitions, week to week, on who could make the most commission off motorists.

They were really into selling oil.

Alex and I prided ourselves on how little oil we sold. The reason was simple. We would only get a nickel commission per can. We didn't think that was much of an incentive.

It just wasn't worth the oily hassle. If someone needed oil, sure, they would get it, but we weren't going to go out of our way for the nickel like Robbie and Boz.

Those guys even gave themselves with titles depending on how much oil they sold per week. For instance, if someone sold forty-five oils in one week they became a "Knight of Oil." Sixty in a week was "Lord of Oil."

And seventy was "God of Oil!"

One week, Boz, being the competitive bastard that he was, sold seventy-six or some insane amount, which added a whole three dollars and eighty cents extra to his paycheck!

Did these guys need their heads examined, or what? They would walk around, feeling all studly, with their shirt sleeves rolled up, showing off the tattoos that they would draw on each other's arms with permanent markers that designated their rank: "LORD OF OIL!"

Then, under it, it would say the amount of oil they sold (71!).

The tattoos looked real tough, too.

I could understand trying to sell anything else but oil. For all of the other stuff we received ten percent commission. An air cleaner? Yep, those stupid circular paper pieces of junk went for nine bucks (a lot at the time): that's a buck commission! Transmission fluid? Yes, you get thirty cents. A quart of coolant went for three bucks; there's another thirty cents. Maybe, just maybe, by the end of the week, all this crap might add up to enough to pay for horrid liquor store meals.

Alex and I were never as crazed about making a commission as Robbie and Boz; we would only sell stuff if customers needed it. Most of the time, when someone needed oil, I would just yell for Robbie or Boz, and they would race over. They would sell anything they could get their little greasy hands on. They were constantly filling up people's power-steering container an eighth of an inch, when the fluid was already right at the top, and it would end up spilling over the brim and down the sides of the container. Then they'd charge them three bucks.

Customers would be so grateful because Robbie and Boz seemed to really care a lot about their cars and their safety. All Robbie and Boz cared about was beating each other at the end of the week on commission add-ups.

When some poor soul needed just a little water in his overflow container—or possibly none at all—Boz and Robbie would be sure to sell them coolant. At Pep Boys, a whole gallon was three bucks. Klaus sold quarts for three bucks, which was normal for a gas station, expensive. Boz would say:

"You're about a quart low on coolant, sir."

"Well, how much is it?" Sir would ask.

"Three dollars," Boz says, being sure to add, "but three dollars is not a high price to pay to save your engine."

"Well, do you think it could wait till next time? I kind of need this money for lunch. This is all I have."

"No," Boz looks him straight in the eye.

Or Robbie says:

"Your air filter is really dirty, ma'am."

"Really? I think I had that replaced recently."

"Look how dirty it is, ma'am."

Robbie holds it up to the light and the thing is nice and clean except for just a little dust.

"Well, you see, ma'am, that's dirt," Robbie says. "And that dirt can get into your engine, drastically reducing the life span potential of your crankshaft."

"Well," she says, skeptically, "Okay. Throw it in."

Then, Robbie goes into the lube bay to start searching for one. First, he has to look it up in the huge book, and that takes him about ten minutes. He finally finds it in the book, then begins searching for it on a shelf, rifling through all of them, (even the ones that are obviously not it—the ones left over from the '60s, which are in a rarely opened drawer at the bottom). They are enormous, larger than wedding cakes, and Klaus refuses to throw them out even though they are from long extinct cars that will never roam the earth again.

Not it. Robbie goes back through all of them, three or four times, from the top. He finally figures out: that we don't have that particular air filter! Then he begins to search for one that he might possibly be able to cram in there. With practically every single air filter out of its box, he finally finds one he thinks will fit. He holds the old air filter up to the new one, comparing diameter and height. Diameter difference, only an inch; and height, just a bit too tall, quarter inch. No matter. He walks over to the car, and begins to try to cram it in. He can. Sold!

Brake fluid was another consumer's nightmare. Boz and Rob would use fear tactics to sell a squirt for three bucks.

"Well, ma'am, you are low on brake fluid, and you could possibly wait till next time, but I wouldn't recommend it. Your brakes could go out on you."

"Oh, no. Please! Put it in!"

Although it sounds like Rob and Boz were assholes, they weren't that bad, just potential 80's style yuppies in training.

It was late June now, and the beach was getting really hot. Most days, the temperature was in the nineties and cars were overheating with more frequency. There was a certain breed of driver who would pull in, car overheating—gurgling, shaking and steaming—but they didn't have the time or patience to let the car cool down, so they would pay the price.

One Step Beyond

It was ninety-five degrees outside, and calculating exponentially, that makes the Monza 4,500 degrees.

They will not wait for it to cool down.

In a situation like this, the grease monkey puts the red rag on the radiator cap, and turns it to the first click to let off some steam. Only the first click, though. This is important. That will let off some of the pressure, and it won't explode in his face.

The problem, though: It's already on the first click - before he started twisting!

Voila! Insta-Death-Geyser! A scalding rebounder off the hood and back down onto the head, which now he can call his "foreRED!"

Sometimes the customer would get too impatient and just wouldn't listen.

A businessman pulls up in his boring four-door American sedan; it's overheating. He wants me to put water in, "Now."

I tell him he should wait for it to cool down a bit first. "No." He wants water, "Now!"

"Okay," I say, reluctantly. "But you have to turn the car on for me to put the water in, 'cause it's too hot."

"I'm not turning this car on!" he says, defensively. "It's way too goddamn hot as it is!"

"But, sir," I say, "you have to turn it on for me to put the water in, 'cause, if you don't, the cold water rushing in all at once is going to crack the block."

"Crack the block? I'm not turning this car on. It's way too hot! Just add the water."

"But, sir, I'm warning you, your engine block is going to crack!"

"I said, just put it in, young man."

"Okay, sir."

So I stick the hose into the radiator and the water starts flowing, and—"CLUNK!"

"What was that?" he asks, alarmed.

"That was the sound of your engine cracking, sir."

"Goddamn it! You're responsible for this! You're going to pay for this!"

Then comes the good part: "But sir, I hate to tell you this ... but I told you so."

"Goddamn it! @&^$#@!$#!%$"

One Step Beyond

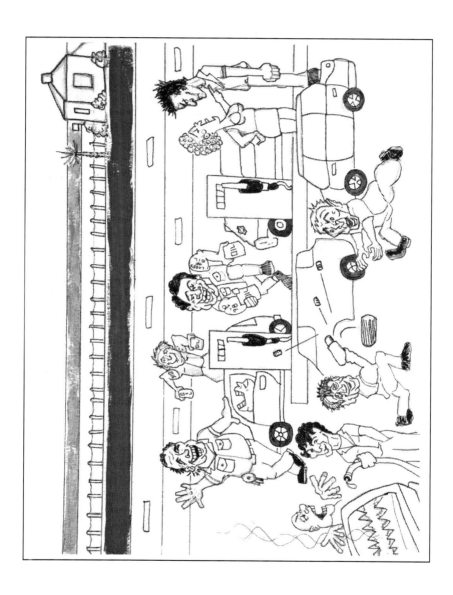

At 9:30 p.m. I start closing up the gas station. I was in charge of closing now. Klaus trusted me, and I could manage okay at night without help. Eddie and Klaus both left at around six. I made sure I locked everything. The day had been long enough, twelve hours. My friends and I were going to meet and hang out at Robbie's. Maybe there'd be some food there...and Amy.

I wasn't living in as much of a fantasy world anymore as far as she went. The thermostat to my brain had started to open and cool water entered and the temperature was receding, not cracking my blockhead. This was good. I had been too preoccupied with her for a couple months.

This night the final dose of cold water came rushing in, freeing me from my intensely frustrating obsession.

Alex, Jeff, Robbie, Boney, and I were in the living room eating and watching TV. At various times throughout the evening I tried making friendly casual contact with Amy, but it was no use; she was preoccupied with something, with someone.

She was making seemingly destination-less trips around the house on this hot night. She was dressed skimpily, in white summer shorts and a light revealing cotton top. We couldn't help but check her out, except for Alex; he wasn't paying attention, as usual. He was probably well aware of her attempts to wet his appetite, but he had the aloof thing going full blast.

We stood around the kitchen for about an hour eating, talking about cars, waves, and music. Then we went to the living room to kick back. It was then that Amy appeared at the top of the stairs in a sexy top, which was casually draping open, on purpose, and she had no bra underneath. The top was open just enough to give any teenage boy cornea damage. I tried to keep sane by not paying too much attention to her, but I knew something was up. She was brewing something, exactly what, I didn't know. After slinking around for a few moments, she disappeared into her room. A couple minutes later, we heard her call down to Alex from the landing.

She said, "Alex, I want to show you something. Come here."

We all looked at each other, stunned. Alex looked around at us, soberly; like he just received a draft notice and he had to go off to war and was certain he wasn't coming back.

He began to ascend the stairs.

My friends and I looked at each other; our faces had the look of bewilderment:

Oh, my God!

Later on, he told me he had entered her room and found her sitting on the side of her bed. Glancing up at him seductively, she began nonchalantly leafing through her yearbook. There she was, legs crossed, revealing her thighs and breasts. It was her idea of being enormously sexy. It was working—for me, that is.

Alex paid good attention to the tour she gave him through her boring yearbook; he said stupid things like: "Oh, I was in Mr. Butt's class."

Then after they spent about fifteen tedious minutes leafing through the yearbook, her emotions welled up and she finally broke down in tears.

"I don't see what you don't like about me? Don't you find me attractive?"

She gripped his hand firmly, and he replied,

"Uh ... uh, yeah ... yeah, uh, I do, but...but..."

Then before he could do anything, she grabbed his hand and put it on one of her breasts and started kissing him like a madwoman. He struggled with the concept. He struggled with the reality of the situation, and then, finally, he just pulled away and walked out.

I found that hard to grasp, or not grasp? Why did he want to leave there so desperately?

She was Robbie's little sister. So they said.

I guess he just didn't want to deal with it. I could respect that, but I couldn't understand it.

While all this was happening, my jealous and immature friends and I (I being the most jealous but possibly not the most immature) congregated outside on the driveway under her second story window. We stood there like sniveling dorks, throwing lemons against her bedroom wall. While we heaved the lemons, we stood in judgment and commented on how Robbie's sister was just way too young, and immature, and, "Why was Alex up there?"

We also asked the question of, "Will Alex get together with her?" The answer we came up with was, "Of course, he shouldn't!"

However, our actions told a different story. We looked like sexually aggravated prehistoric adolescents, heaving the projectiles at the fortress, subconsciously shouting:

"WE WANT THE GIRL! WE WANT THE GIRL! GIVE US THE GIRL!"

If Alex did go for it, though, we were going to give him a lot of shit! I knew what I'd do. My friends had to be thinking the same thing.

The minutes ticked by like hours for us. Then, finally, we hypocrites watched Alex walk slowly out of the house. He looked dazed, as though he had seen a ghost. His head was darting back and forth nervously, swiveling in different directions. He was trying to look casual with his hands in his pockets, but it wasn't working. He looked spooked.

He said nothing happened, and I believed him. Now, I'm not quite so sure.

Either way, there would always be more attractive girls for Alex. I was so envious of him. Women just loved him.

When Alex was in eleventh grade, one of the most popular and gorgeous girls in the school liked him. She was a twelfth-grader. She was the girl that every guy at some point in school lost his mind over. She was a blonde babe who was hot, smart, and classy.

Alex would sit there, like no big deal, talking to her every day in algebra. She sat in front of him. One day the word got around school that she liked him. At the start of nutrition, he walked over to his usual group of friends and they let him have it. One kid blurted out:

"I can't believe Diana Mayfield likes you! Oh, my God! You don't even understand. I've been going crazy for her every single second since elementary school, and you..."

Just then she walked up.

"Hi, Alex," she said, with her nine hundred watt smile. All the guys were just staring at her with serious, blank, expressions on their faces.

Then she said to Alex, "Can I talk to you privately for a sec."

He went walking off with her about twenty feet away from the group. His friends were completely quiet, watching over their shoulders, straining to hear.

She said she needed help with algebra and could he tutor her ... at her house, tonight?

And he said, "Uh ... you know ... uh, I'm really not that good at algebra. You know, uh, you should really get David Miller, because that guy always gets A's. I only get B's. Yeah, I'm really not that good at algebra."

Then she said: "No, you're good at it. Please."

He tried to argue his way out of it some more. Finally, after she wouldn't take no for an answer, he said, okay, and he gave her his number.

He walked back to the group of guys and they were all standing there dumbfounded and pissed off. One kid barked at him:

"What? What was that? What did she want?"

Without any sense of excitement and with hardly any expression, he said, "She wants me to come over and tutor her in math. She wants me to come over to her house tonight."

Another guy stood there with his mouth open. A distraught expression unfolded across his face, as he said: "You fucking dick!"

Alex went over to her house, night after night. Guess what happened? He tutored her in algebra!

On the first day of spring semester, 11th grade, Alex was sitting in a class waiting for it to start. The bell was just about to ring. People around him were staking out their permanent semester-long seats. Alex was sitting with Jeff and Boz when he saw a beautiful girl, Emma, sitting on the other side of the classroom. Emma caught Alex's eye and waved him over.

"Alex, come over here."

She pointed to an empty seat next to her. He picked up his stuff, walked over, sat down and began chatting with her. A moment later, four of the most attractive girls in the school shuffled in, smiling, saying hi to Emma and some others; and they all took seats on every side of Alex. He was surrounded, surrounded by beautiful young women. Then, at that second, the bell rang. Everyone was locked into his or her seats for the whole semester.

Alex looked back over his shoulder to his friends, and they had these horrified deserted looks on their faces. Their expressions said "Banished" to the other side of the class with the nerds and geeks.

It was like Siberia over there and it was only fourteen feet away. They stared back at him like puppies being asphyxiated. They couldn't believe it.

That was basically how it was all the way through high school for Alex. Mostly, he just liked the attention and the esteem boost of these situations. That was good enough for him. Every now and then he would get himself into a fix by getting together with a girl, but he'd quickly remedy the situation by never calling, or, when they'd call him, he'd just mumble nonsense into the phone pretending that they woke him up from taking a nap. He'd tell them, "I caw yu bak, ohay?" When he never did and he saw them later, he'd use the old mystical, "Wow. No way. I don't even remember you calling," excuse.

Emma was crazy about Alex. She made her final attempt at the high school graduation ceremony. It was the last day in which they all would be together, the last day before they would go off to different colleges, different lives, and in many cases never see each other again. It was the major turning point in their lives so far.

Everyone was in cap and gown, and they were on their way, walking down through a tunnel that led to steps to the school's football field where the ceremony was about to begin. On one side of the steps was a steep ivy slope. Emma was walking arm in arm with Alex in the middle of a group of friends. Many people in the class had managed to smoke pot or drink hard liquor from little hidden flasks at some time during the morning. Emma was sauced. As she walked down the stairs with Alex she "accidentally" fell and pulled him into the ivy bed with her. In front of everyone she began to kiss him madly. He lay there, stunned, with her on top of him, not really knowing what to do. He wasn't fighting it. He was kind of waiting there in a way, waiting for her to come to her senses? He was moving his head back and forth from side to side, avoiding her kisses, and all the students just watched and laughed as they marched by. He kissed her back a little bit, politely, while calmly saying,

"Emma, you're drunk ... Em-ma."

She kept on kissing him.

One Step Beyond

It seemed so easy for him. I was so jealous I could have died. I wished that I had that kind of response from girls. I just wasn't that kind of guy; I was too nice, too transparent and available when I liked a girl. To make matters worse I was too insecure and fearful of rejection to just go up and meet them. Alex would remain single and satisfied during the time we worked at the gas station. I was single and frustrated.

I was determined to get a girlfriend. I didn't know any girls, though.

There was one girl who I thought was very cute. I used to see her sitting at the bus stop at the far end of the station on the side of the liquor store. She would go to the beach almost every day, then wait until four o'clock for the bus to come take her home. I guess she met her friends at the beach but always took the bus alone. She looked about sixteen, elegant, waiting for the Blue Bus, a serene expression on her face, her beautiful, tan legs crossed. She was petite, about 5'2" had straight short hair, which was just coming back into style for girls, probably for the first time since the flapper era. I grew up in the seventies and girls always had long hair.

She was beautiful and modern.

I didn't have the nerve to talk to her. I thought about starting up a conversation with her by saying things like, "Waiting for the bus?"

Or: "Would you care for a bite of my liquor-store burrito? Watch out for the cartilage nugget chunks."

Or: "Could I give you a ride home in my serial killer automobile? You might make it home alive."

Or maybe just: "Hi, my name's Mike. I take a trip to the liquor store daily around this time just so I can drool over you."

"Forget it." I did.

I shouldn't have. A few years later I realized that it doesn't really matter what you say to start up a conversation as long as you say it without thinking, or worrying about it too much. For instance, I could have just said, "Hi. I'm a gas station worker. See the grease all over my body? Grease is the word, you know. Wanna do it?" Sure, I could've said that.

I headed back from the liquor store for the millionth time and took a good look at my dream girl but was too afraid to make eye contact. If she did happen to look up, what would I do? Smile? No way, I was too unnerved by her.

When I came back to reality, I saw that the Snap-on truck was parked in front of the station's lube bay. It was a shiny truck loaded with nice expensive tools for sale. All the guys crowded around the truck, caressing the gleaming new Snap-on tools. They were completely mesmerized by the objects. I never got too excited about those things.

Eddie was always first to the truck, running over with his pants slipping down as he tugs them back up, his keys jangling on his belt, "Hey, Buddy! That ratchet I got from you the other day is fucking killer."

Klaus heard all the commotion and emerged from his little office. He squints, spots the guy and yells:

"Get that ahsole out of here!"

Eddie would then spend an hour-and-a-half bullshitting with the guy, buying more and more tools each time. He was addicted.

As the guys drooled over a torque wrench, a disturbed woman pulled in to get gas.

I walked over to help her.

She was having a hard time with self-serve. She appeared agitated and confused, standing there with the pump in her hand, unable to get gas. I walked over and flipped the lever down for her as she inserted the nozzle into her car.

She looked over at me with a hateful glare, then walked back over to the pump and flipped the lever back up. She had just turned it off. The gas would not flow now. I inserted the key to reset it. I said nothing, 'cause I was bored and tired, and I flipped the lever back up. The pump was ready again.

Then, with a furious look, she walked toward me, and flipped the lever back up again, turning it off.

I walked over and did the key thing once again. I flipped it and said calmly, "Don't flip the lever, because then you won't be able to get any gas."

She screamed at me at the top of her lungs and I jumped back.

"Goddamn it!" she said. "I don't know how to work this—I've never worked at a goddamn gas station! Shit!" She was losing it.

"I know," I said, getting irritated and defensive right along with her. "That's what Full Serve is for. You can stay in your car, and we'll do it for you."

"I don't work at a gas station!" she screamed. "I can't be expected to know everything!"

Aaaagghh! I was getting more upset. I was trying to help her and she was attacking me!

"Hey, lady, I'm trying to help you! Without me you wouldn't be able to get any gas at all! So stop screaming at me ... I'm being nice to you!"

"You're horrible! What's your name?" she said, squinting her eyes. "You're evil. One of the most evil people!"

"No, lady, I'm nice! I'm really nice! Without me you would be nowhere. You would be lost. You wouldn't be able to get any gas—EVER! I'm the nicest person in the world!"

"Nooo!! You're the worst!!! I HATE YOU!!! What's your name? I'm telling your boss!"

"My name's Mike, lady: M-I-K-E. Mike Pearson. M-I-K-E P-E-A-R-S-O-N. And my boss is right inside if you'd like to talk to him all about me and how I'm straight from hell. Be my guest. Because I'm nice! Very Fucking Nice!!

"AAGGH!!!" she screamed, as she marched into the lube-bay looking for Klaus.

A moment later, he came out with serious purpose, pointing at me.

"Is that him?" he asked her.

"Yes, that's him," she said, huffing and puffing. She tried to catch her breath as she explained to Klaus how I could strike again. How I could do it again, again.

One Step Beyond

Then Klaus lowered his voice and spoke to her very seriously:

"Yes. He is very bad. This has happened before. And yes, he could strike again. Yes, he could. He will be punished, there is no doubt, and he will definitely be punished."

I stood there, quietly, acting upset, like, Damn, I'm going to be fired.

"Yes. He will definitely be fired." Klaus continued. "You are fired, Mr. Pearson. Pick up your paycheck on Friday. You will receive no pay for today." I walked away. I walked over to the beach, pretending to be sad, and actually I was. It was depressing to me. I stayed at the beach for a while trying to get some kind of peace back. I told my parents about it that night, and they just laughed. It was funny, but it was also sad and harsh. How do people get so messed up like that? I hated the woman but I also felt sorry for her. She must act like like that all the time. How did she become that way? Had she been abused or neglected as a child? Could it be biological? I thought about those who she might have affected in all of her days on earth. I wondered if she had children. It was just sad. What do you do with people like that? Help them, avoid them, love them, hate them, fear them? I was confused and disturbed by it.

Mike Pearson

One Step Beyond

Deep Summer
The Canyon Kid Men Of Rustic
& Various Other Sick Puppies
"Wasted" by Black Flag

There were these guys who lived in Rustic Canyon who hung around the station. I called them The Canyon Kid Men of Rustic. They weren't men, but they weren't kids either. They were both. They were in their mid-twenties to early-thirties and still lived in the 1970s; they weren't changing with the times (or if they were, it was too slow a process to detect). Their lives were all about surfing, smoking pot, and screwing chicks ... not a terrible life, but you'd think on occasion they'd wear something other than a coarse, ratty, hooded, Mexican sweatshirt, swim trunks and flip flops.

After awhile, their clothes did start to change with the times. For instance, by the late-eighties some of them would start wearing fluorescent clothing and neon fanny-packs that faced forward on the waist, and some of them even gave in and cut their hair; but no matter what, they would still hold onto that one thing that, at least, symbolically, comfortingly, connected them to their pot-soothed '70s past: their mustache!

They were roofers, floor men, gardeners who called themselves landscapers, painters, construction workers, and craftsmen. Mainly, they lived to surf, surfed to live, and smoked a lot of dope.

My first encounter with them was years earlier in junior high when I was first learning to surf. They would paddle over, quickly and aggressively, and sit right next to me, with stoned smiles on their faces, hooting and hollering, singing '70s rock songs, taking off in front of me, before I could turn my board around. They'd be singing "Feel Like Making Love" by Bad Company, or Foreigner's "Cold as Ice," or Foghat's "Fool for the City," crap like that. A lot of these guys were mean bastards, too, in and out of the water, gruelers, for the most part. They would come by and tell us how fucked chicks were and that they were good for only one thing. I remember one of them being really nice; he drove a big, old, orange American car and sold toys out of it. He always had toys packed up to the roof in that thing. He was a clown for kids' parties. Another guy, Bob Nhon, would come in at night and fix his car. He'd brag to us about how the night before, he boned this girl in his car on his disgusting, sandy, multi-colored Mexican blanket (the kind that surfers always buy when down in Baja) and he told us how he had to put the seats forward in order to "do her just right."

"Yeah, braghh, dude, you should've seen this honey I had last night. Man! Long legs spread from door to door. She was rad, man, you should've seen her!" I responded to that: "Hey, man, you should clean that blanket."

These guys were so grungy. Most of them lived in converted garages behind their parents' houses. I don't think they ever took showers. They probably figured since they surfed every morning, the ocean was their bath. They shaved about twice a week. They didn't have a lot of cash, and never bought over two dollars worth of gas at any one time. Needless to say, they came in constantly to fill up their tanks.

We'd see them a lot at night after Klaus had gone home. They would put their cars up on the hydraulic lift and do oil changes and repairs, without ever asking, of course. They had all worked at the station at one time or other and in their minds it gave them lifelong access to Klaus's lifts. I always worried that one day their cars would fall off on their heads because they were always so stoned when they'd put them up there. They smoked dope at the beach all day long; they smoked dope in their car in our parking lot; they'd definitely smoked dope at a "day party." They'd be smoking out by the dumpster:

"Wanna hit, man?" Cough, cough. "Give me a puff, dude.... SSSSwwwwwww. Hhehehhh!" Cough, cough. "I'm okay, all right, dude, cool, let's party... Cool now, bro, all right, let's surf, get a six pack, cool, score some more buds, let's call Skip." Skip was the dealer.

The Kid Men made me nervous. I always wanted to tell them that smoking pot and putting a car ten feet up in the air doesn't always mix, but they would've probably just punched me hard in my chest. This was not an irrational fear, because, as a kid out in the water surfing, if you took off on one of their waves, they'd certainly paddle right up to you fast and punch you right in the chest before you even knew what happened.

"Dick!" they'd bark as they slammed their knuckles into your chest. The Canyon Kid Men were cool as long as you didn't try to take their waves, their buds or their babes.

Actually, the Kid Men made me VERY nervous, not so much because they might punch me, but because I worried about ending up like them. I was already like them in many ways. I longed for more direction. I just didn't know where to find it.

The Fourth of July arrived and it was the wildest, most hectic, day of the year at the gas station. By noon, the highway was at a standstill, packed with thousands of cars. It seemed everyone had to go to the beach on the 4th and get wasted. Every inch of the gas station lot was packed with parked cars. All the cars were parked one foot apart; the only place where they weren't parked was a narrow path for vehicles to pull in and out of the station in Full-Serve, where they had to serve themselves, because we were too busy drinking beer and parking cars.

"That guy's overheating!"

"Get that guy's parking money. He's getting away!"

"Shit, that kid just lit an M-250 ... There! Right next to you—Watch it!"

It was a circus from morning to midnight. Fireworks would come sailing right up to us, and we'd hurl them back. At a gas station! Explosives!

The place turned into pure anarchy and we had to kind of groove with it or else we would go completely nuts along with everyone else. It was funny because at the height of anarchy even Klaus didn't seem to care what happened. Most of our carefree attitude came from drinking the cases of German beer Klaus's friend had dropped off. My friends and I were pretty sauced and we were parking all the cars.

Robbie and Boz didn't even know how to drive automatic cars let alone sticks, let alone drunk. If a person ever wanted out of a parking space, we'd have to move about thirty cars so he could get out.

Robbie was the worst driver of us all. He tried to park a skinny gay guy's Volvo. The man pulled his colorful cloth beach chair out of the trunk, had his bag in his hand, and was walking toward the beach. Right then, Robbie slipped and popped his clutch and the car flew forward and bounced off the car in front of it. The owner heard it, tensed his shoulders up, looked back, gritting his teeth, as Robbie kept grinding his gears violently trying to force it into reverse. I don't know why Klaus let Robbie park cars.

One morning, I made the mistake of letting Robbie drive me surfing. I figured, "Hey, this will be nice. I'll be able to relax, let someone else drive for a change."

Relax? Yeah, right! I was mentally making out my last will and testament as we flew down the road at six in the morning. Robbie had a little, yellow Chevette. We were heading down P.C.H. and approaching Kanan Dume road when the light turned yellow. The speed limit was forty-five and the yellow lights last three and a half hours. But what did he do? He thought it was to be red real soon, so he slammed the breaks fifteen feet from the intersection. What did he think the yellow was for? We ended up sliding sideways, wildly, for a long time. We finally came to a halt, diagonally, in the middle of the intersection, under the traffic light, which hung above our heads. I sat there facing forward, serene as a dead person who just had his dick cut off. I didn't say anything, no expression. A couple of hour-long seconds passed. It was too damn early for me with this kind of shit. I looked up, and above my head, the light quietly blinked red. There was a car waiting on a side street with a person in it who was shaking their head in disbelief. They wanted to go but we were blocking the intersection. Robbie wasn't sure what to do? Go backward? Forward? It was a real dilemma. I rotated my neck to the left, looked him straight in the eye, and screamed at the top of my lungs: "GO! YOU ASSHOLE!!" Then he fumbled and squeezed the cheesy Chevette shifter into first and snailed his way off toward Zuma.

It was August now, and there was a heat wave with several hundred-degree-days. It seemed somehow that the heat brought on an increase in the amount of lunatics visiting the station. It also seemed to be making them more deranged and volatile. There were a variety of maniacs. One day Alex and I were filling up cars as Jeff walked up. He looked nervous but was trying to keep his cool. "Hey, you guys, come over here," he said, quietly. "This weirdo's prying open Klaus's door."

We leaned around the corner just enough to get a peek. A serious dirt-bag was trying to pry open Klaus's office door. He was jostling at the door with crusty, old butter-knives. At that moment he looked over and stared at us. He had a demented look in his eyes, as he held up the butter knives and showed them to us with his teeth bared, eyes wild, like a rabid animal. We didn't know what to do. Just then, he broke his glare from us, turned and darted out of there. Brrrrrrrrr. He ran up the coast highway. We were glad, too, because we weren't exactly in the mood for a fight in which we got stabbed with dirty butter knifes.

A couple weeks later we saw someone prying at Klaus's door again. It was another nervous freaked-out dude and he was using a screwdriver. Alex walked over to him, casually, having become familiar with this kind of situation by now, and said, "May I help you?"

The nervous dude turned to him, sweating, fidgeting, then he mumbled, partly to himself, pretending to be casual, "I'm just trying to sharpen my screwdriver here. Uh ... it's a little dull."

This stumped Alex. He didn't know what to do. They looked at each other, with bizarre expressions, for a long moment. Then Alex motioned to him, "here," and hesitantly led him over to the bench grinder—to sharpen his screwdriver!

They were at the bench grinder and Alex reached out for the screwdriver, and the man handed to him. Alex was sharpening the screwdriver for the crazy man, and they stayed there for a few tense moments. Alex's mind was racing and his heart pounding as he helped the man grind down his screwdriver to a nice sharp point. Then, after a long sharpening, Alex felt that the time had come to give it back to him. He hesitated at first, then he quickly handed it back to him, as he took two quick steps back; the freak glared at him, grabbed it out of his hand and darted off like the maniac that he was.

Alex called the cops and reported that a weirdo was on foot heading down the coast armed with an extremely sharp screwdriver. We learned later that the police were rarely interested in this kind of thing. The rule of thumb was that they needed blood to spill before it could become a priority.

Klaus didn't rely on the police, though. He had an old baseball bat that he kept propped up in the corner near the windshield wiper blades. It had check marks on it, about ten of them from when Klaus supposedly used it.

I asked Klaus, "Are the check marks from every time you hit somebody with it or just every time you had to threaten somebody with it?" He evaded the question but I like to think it depended on how hairy the confrontation was before the bat earned a check.

Klaus treated us to a bat story.

Klaus: "One time some ahsole comes in and tries to steal some tools and."

"What kind of tools? I asked."

"I don't know, some fucking wrenches, Michael, I don't remember."

"Expensive ones?"

"I don't know, just some fucking tools. Okay, expensive ones, if you like it that way, they're all fucking expensive ... That goddamn Snap On guy..."

"Okay, Klaus: the bat," I put him back on track.

"So, he was trying to steal some tools." Klaus paused. "The ahsole was on his way running out of the lube-bay with his arms filled with tools, so I grab the bat and I hit him and the tools go flying all over the place and then I take this ..." Then Klaus went over to the hydraulic car lift and demonstrated by opening the control valve; the lift started going up.

"And I pin the ahsole underneath the lift." Then Klaus showed how he lowered it onto him. "And I hold him there till the cops come and take him away."

"No way, Klaus. Really?"

"Really, yeah." he said, "'Ahsole, get under the lift!'"

"Really, Klaus?"

Then Klaus said, in a hippie-gone-bad accent,

"'Oh, come on, Man.' I said, 'Now, ahsole!' 'OWH...maann.' 'That's what you get, Ahsole.'"

Jeff seemed to get stuck with the most severe gas station maniacs. An old, beat-up, four-door American sedan pulled up and Jeff went over to the driver's window to say "fill it up?' and in the back seat driver-side he saw a young woman sitting there sobbing. She looked traumatized and in shock. The back windows were dirty and rolled up, and Jeff couldn't see too well. He ducked down a little as he inserted the pump nozzle so he could get a peek in the back. The woman looked sick and pale, and sitting next to her was a ratty, unshaven, dirty, greasy man repeatedly poking her with a knife, with small quick pokes! He was doing this over and over. Was he trying to keep her from screaming? This didn't seem like a very nice way. Who knew how long he'd been doing this? Long enough, Jeff figured, because she was on the bloody and tender side at this point. Jeff could see about a six-inch blood splotch on the side of her blouse. In the front of the car two serious-looking scruffy men faced forward, silent, as the gas went in, they looked to be in their thirties, they looked haggard and trashy. The sicko in back was not stabbing her deeply; it was just with the tip of the blade, but consistently. He wouldn't stop, and she looked very weak.

As the car filled with gas, Jeff went inside and told Klaus. Klaus came out with the baseball bat in his hand.

"All right, ahsole! Get the fuck out of the car!" Klaus opened the back passenger side rear door and pulled the man out of the car. Then the car sped away with the girl and the two men that were in front.

Alex got the license number and Klaus called the cops. Klaus put the sicko in the small front room that had the maps and pay phone. Jeff's job description now included guarding maniacs. Klaus gave Jeff the baseball bat and told him to guard the maniac until the police got there. He then ordered Alex and Robbie to keep pumping gas because it was rush hour, which meant prime business hour. Klaus went back into his office, continuing to add up credit card slips, while checking every now and then through the one-way mirror to make sure Jeff hadn't been killed.

Alert and nervous, Jeff stood guard, looking like it was the last thing in the world he wanted to be doing. He gripped the bat in his hand. The maniac sat there sweating, fidgeting and giving off a creepy vibe while waiting for the law to come.

After sitting there for ten minutes, the prisoner started to get impatient; he made a move to get up from the chair and Jeff screamed at him:

"No! You sit!"

He sat, resentfully, crossing his legs, like a scolded French artist. A few more minutes went by and the maniac started shifting in his chair again. He began to get up.

Jeff was intent on keeping his ward, and raised the bat up to scare the guy. There was no help to be had for Jeff, though; everyone was too busy checking under hoods, pumping gas and filling out credit card slips.

Jeff screamed aggressively, "Sit down!" The maniac sat back down again.

One Step Beyond

"Okay, okay," he grumbled.

A minute or so later the maniac stood up defiantly and pulled out a sharp, bloody-tipped steak knife, and with a crazed glare in his eye he began to move toward Jeff. How could they have forgotten to take the knife away?

Jeff lifted the bat and rushed at the maniac, yelling at the top of his lungs.

"Aagghh! Put the knife on the ground!"

Obediently he sat back down in his chair, tossed the knife on the floor and grumbled,

"Okay, okay."

The cops arrived a moment or two later and took him away. I imagine they locked him up for about fifteen minutes before giving him back his steak knife and wishing him good luck. We laughed about that one for a long time. We thought it was so funny: Jeff having to guard a homicidal maniac by himself, and he got $3.50 an hour for that!

One Step Beyond

***

Then there were the small time swindlers and the tricksters.

There was one type in particular whom I called the Change Trickster. Most cashiers have come across this one at least once in their career.

Here's an example:

A tall, skinny, guy comes in. He's wearing a baseball cap; sweat pants and a Lakers T-shirt. He wants change for a $20, but he also wants to pay for his $4.50 worth of gas with another $20.

This bamboozle has tricked many.

He wants to pay you $4.50, he wants change for that and the twenty but he also needs change for a five, but then you think I might as well split his ten into two fives, and then he has to give you back this much, but now you owe him another five because of the two bucks he gave you earlier, and so on, and so on. Confusing, huh? Well, it's supposed to be. He tries doing this until you have no idea how much money you're losing and how much he should get, and you just start giving him all kinds of money, because you have no idea what the fuck is going on anymore. Anyway, that's how it's supposed to work. I had already experienced dudes like this and had heard all the stories from Eddie and Klaus, so I was ready. I went through the whole process with him, making all the transactions, playing dumb the whole time, like I really understood why he needs so many different types of change, because the video games and the burrito, and he's got to call his old woman, etc. I follow his every move. The bastard thinks he has me. The whole time I'm acting like an idiot, "Oops ... duh." He thinks I'm losing money. He walks away confused in the end. He didn't know how much he got out of me, but he was sure he got something, maybe even a lot. Later, the Change Trickster realized, I ripped him off five bucks.

Then there were the Watch Leavers. They leave watches for us to hold when they don't have any money and they need gas. Mostly the watches are only worth about 50 cents, and it's a scam to get a full tank of gas. To Robbie, however, they look like they're worth three thousand dollars. The Watch Leavers don't come back with money to pay up. Their cheapo watch sits in the cash register for years as a testament to the idiocy of a long forgotten employee.

Sometimes we'd take their driver's licenses as collateral and when they wouldn't come back we'd use them as fake IDs, trying to pass ourselves off as bald forty-five-year-old Iranians.

Every now and then, someone would leave a watch actually worth a thousand dollars because their car really was stranded on the coast highway blocking up traffic and they had no cash but needed to borrow a gas can. Later, they would drive in to pay up and be reunited with their Rolex and at that point Klaus would be there, playing dumb.

"Hi," the man says. "I just came back to get my watch."

"You're not the guy who left that watch, are you? We just gave that Rolex back to its rightful owner, that black man; that Hispanic man who was just here. That was his watch, right? Sir? That was his watch? Wasn't it...?

The customer starts going crazy, and Klaus lets him throw a fit for a few minutes, then Klaus begins to smile, letting the guy know he's screwing with his head.

One Step Beyond

"All right, I got your fucking watch." Klaus says, as a constipated smile forms across the guy's face in relief that Klaus is such a kidder.

Klaus loved to drive people crazy. When it came to directions, he was possibly at his worst. He'd give them the wrong directions on purpose just to watch them squirm. You could see the wheels of their brain spinning, as they grappled with the idea of how far off they were, and they were so confused. How could they ever go so wrong? How could they be a hundred and fifty miles from Malibu? Then he would either tell them the correct directions or just walk away shaking his head, mumbling, "Dumbfuck."

Then I'd end up telling them the right directions. Trying to defend Klaus would not be easy. I didn't know why I bothered.

"He's not as big of an asshole as he seems."

A station wagon with a large family pulled in. They had been going the wrong way for twenty miles. They wanted Knott's Berry Farm.

Klaus said, "48 miles. Straight up the coast."

I told them, "No. He's kidding; you need to go back."

I was always too helpful for my own good; I'd end up spending ages with these people, leading them over to the map, trying to convince them that it's east they wanted and not west. It was frustrating because a lot of the time they were disoriented and in denial and refused to believe it when I told them they had been going the wrong way for almost an hour.

I understood how Klaus got sick of giving the right directions. I got sick of it after a few months and he'd been dealing with it for over twenty years.

A car drove right up to Klaus: "Where's Malibu?" Klaus instantly said, "Sir, that is 89 miles, straight up the coast."

"89 miles?"

"Yes, sir."

Klaus would then walk away.

Then I'd say: "No. He's only kidding. It's five miles."

Or: "Where's The Charthouse?"

"Oh, sir," Klaus said. "You passed that 14 miles ago. Big sign on the side of the road up in lights, neon lights. You didn't see it?"

It was actually a few miles up the highway.

Or:

"Where's Gladstone's 4 fish?" and Klaus spits it out at a hundred and fifty miles-per-hour:

"Fifthstoplightlefthandside."

"What?" and they'd watch his flat ass walk away from them.

I was burned out on giving directions and I had even gotten to the point where I wanted to avoid repairs, especially near closing time. A guy might arrive at ten at night with his tires popped. I wanted to go home. I'd been there all day. If Robbie was around I could forget it. He would get excited about repairs. Immediately he'd tell the guy:

"Oh, yeah, Mike'll fix it for ya. Won't you, Mike?"

Victim of Severe Tire Damage would give me that pitiful look.

"Mike ... Help me out?"

I'd end up selling him tires that didn't even fit his car just so he can get back to God knows where. I might end up stuck there till midnight because Robbie got hot and bothered about selling tires. The other problem was that the beach parking lot across the highway had tire spikes that often times nobody knew about until it was too late.

A guy tries to pull into the beach lot at fifty miles per hour because all these jerks are on his ass and he doesn't want them to crash into the back of his Pinto, and he's signaling, but that doesn't matter. They are definitely going to rear end him so he rips into the driveway but he's about three feet too far over to the left. He hits the spikes and his tires explode; and he's screwed because his spare is already on his car. He comes and sees Mike.

The truth was I was getting tired of the gas station in general. I was doing too much for $3.75 an hour and Klaus wouldn't give me a raise. I was starting to resent it. The guys at the other Chevron were making $4.25 and they were just pumping gas. They weren't managing the place at night.

I was thinking about quitting. I would be starting Santa Monica City College in a couple of weeks, and felt I should get serious about school.

It was a Sunday in September, 7 a.m., peaceful and quiet at the station. There was hardly anybody out on the highway. The sun was low in the sky and a nice warm breeze was blowing; everything was starting to warm up. It was just

Diego and I. Diego was sitting on the tailgate of the Ranchero sipping his coffee. I was taking the "Disneyland Kit" around the parking lot and sweeping up little pieces of paper. It looked and felt like a desert. There were all these nice smooth mounds of sand in the corners of the parking lot. Last night's winds had blown it over from the beach. The restaurant owners were setting up, preparing for another hot, loud day at the grill. Their roadhouse sat at the end of our parking lot. Their burgers were good but expensive and they wouldn't give us a neighborly discount. The owner thought I was cute.

He said, "My, how you've grown. You've turned into a real handsome young man."

I'd think to myself, thank you, but what I really want is an affordable burger. I'd also think, if only I could get that kind of response from teenage girls, instead of fifty-year-old men, I'd be set.

At 8 a.m. I was back on the tailgate with Jimmy. We didn't talk much. We sat there peacefully, soaking up the early morning sun. It wasn't going to be long before it turned into another insane day at the beach.

It seemed that only mellow people were out on the road now, people who went to sleep early and woke up early to get a nice, fresh start. No partying the night before. Across the highway the waves were calm, just ripples, and the sand had no marks and everything was quiet. Santa Monica College was on my mind. I'd either have to cut back in a big way on my hours at the station, or quit. I'd been putting my education off for twelve years and it was time to do some studying. I dreaded telling Klaus I was going to quit because I knew he was going to be disappointed, he enjoyed my being there, and he knew good workers were hard to find.

I quit. I felt bad for leaving Klaus and countered my guilty feelings by thinking about how Klaus had taken advantage of me. He expected me to manage the place at night, every night, closing at midnight. This would make doing homework very difficult and would destroy any chance for a social life. Everything the station had to offer me for $3.75 an hour? No way. I could have said no, and try to work a couple of nights a week, but I felt it was better to just quit. I knew I wouldn't be able to hold a boundary with Klaus; he was stubborn and I was malleable. Of course, I was more fortunate than most; I didn't have to work. My parents would give me money so I could just go to school. My friends had quit the station and were applying themselves in school and I felt that I should do the same. It was important for me to do well in college and stop feeling like a slacker; which wasn't good for my already low confidence. I wanted to achieve something in life, though I didn't really know what. All I knew was that I should work hard and transfer to a four-year college as soon as possible.

One Step Beyond

Fall 1982
This Is The Modern World
"The Modern World" by the Jam

A miracle! Immediately upon quitting the gas station I met a group of new friends and life suddenly opened up. I couldn't believe how it just sort of happened. I went from grease monkey to socially popular guy in an instant. It was a mystery to me but felt as simple as opening and closing a door. It all started with Alex. He was at the beach one day and he met a couple girls through a mutual friend, Don Gear. Alex frolicked with the girls out in the water, body surfing and splashing back and forth with them. He described the girls as buoyant babes with big boobs on tight little sixteen-year-old bodies. He told me that Don Gear was throwing a party at his parents' house and that these girls and their friends would be there. We went to Gear's big house on the cliff overlooking the ocean (a five minute walk from my house). I was introduced to all the girls, and also a bunch of cool and friendly new dudes. We made screwdrivers and drank those and a bunch of Lowenbrau's and listened to The Jam and The Specials and talked about interesting things.

I was the only one who was out of high school. I felt old comparatively, but I was only seventeen. The girls were in tenth and eleventh grade. They were all attractive, and they impressed me, they were intelligent and interesting to me. They liked to talk about current issues, politics, music, etc., and they were very friendly! I had hit the mother lode! I was so excited! I didn't know people like this existed. They certainly didn't come out of the schools I went to. They were from "alternative" and private schools.

Don Gear was the man. He was a warm, friendly guy who was upbeat and always smiling. He was 5' 9", with thick, puffy blond hair, and he had a little belly. We called him Gear Bear, as well as Kaboobie. He used to call me Kaboobie, too. We got to know each other back when we were video game addicts back in the tenth grade. We were obsessed with an enigmatic older guy who had devised a pattern for Pac Man that enabled him to achieve hundreds of thousands of points (multiple "keys") and outrageous high scores. We played around, pretending that we were in total awe of him, too afraid to speak to him. We could only stand back and watch him rip the game apart. He was a holy man. Don managed to get the nerve and ask him his name and if he would (please!) show us his game pattern.

He replied, "My name is Kaboobie, and this is my pattern. I will teach it to you, but you must always remember, it is my pattern—Kaboobie's pattern." We had nothing but respect for Kaboobie. I think we wanted to be Kaboobie—maybe that's why we called each other Kaboobie.

Don Gear Kaboobie's house was big and beautiful, around five thousand square feet, six enormous bedrooms, a pool, Jacuzzi and a tennis court. I knew every inch of this house. In elementary school I used to hang out with the kid who had lived there before Gear. He was a hyperactive and angry child. His dad was the Postmaster General—a busy man who was never home. There was a wall of nine TVs in the basement that would baby-sit the kid while daddy was gone. He could watch them all at the same time if he desired. For the last few years, Don called it home.

Don had just started going out with Audrey, one of the buoyant ones whom he met with Alex at the beach. She was really charming. Even though she was in love with Gear, I had a massive crush on her. I would borrow her and talk for hours, mostly asking her about girls and how they thought. At that point, I'd spent so much time with guys—surfing, skateboarding, punk rock, cars, motorcycles because of my paralyzing fear of women, that I was behind and needed to learn as much as possible, quickly.

Gear walked up while I was talking to Audrey. He stood there smiling.

I looked at him and said, "Hey, Kaboobie."

"Kaboobie!" he yelled back at me.

"Kaboobie, you're awesome and your girlfriend's rad," I said.

"No, Kaboobie, you're the man. You're the Pac Man! Slurpin'em up! Slurpin'em up, Kaboobie!"

"Hey, Kaboobie, how can I get a girl like Audrey?"

"The Pattern, Kaboobs. Use the Pattern."

"Oh, yeah."

The kids we met at Gear's party were into the recent revival of the mod and ska music scene, which first came about in the early '60s. The movie Quadrophenia depicted mods and rockers during the sixties. The second wave started in England in the late seventies and was just becoming popular, and trendy around the beach communities of Southern California in '82. Some of the more well known second-wave English bands were The Jam, The Specials, English Beat, Madness, Body Snatchers, Selector, and Bad Manners. In Los Angeles, the most popular band was the Untouchables who began to pull more and more people into the scene and into their high energy, amazing shows.

I loved the way ska mixed the intensity of punk with the spirit of soul and vibe of reggae. I also liked that the music was upbeat and got people dancing. The music was upbeat, but the lyrics were also thoughtful and progressive. All in all, it was a great new experience to be a part of.

I thought the dancing was cool. I liked that people danced with each other instead of just spinning in their own spaced-out worlds like hippies of the previous fifteen years. The clothes always looked smart. Guys would wear early '60s style, sleek tapered suits, with thin ties, thin lapels. It was the antithesis of the seventies or even current 80's fashion, where everything was big, wide, and garish and over the top. The mod girls wore cute outfits found at second hand stores or their grand parents closets. Boys and girls were clean cut with short hair. Mods often wore big green army parkas with targets on the back or the iconic skanking man (skanking was a style of dancing). Most of them rode vintage Lambretta and Vespa scooters with lots of mirrors, like the early 60s mods in Quadrophenia.

The '80s were in full effect. Everything felt and looked different. People were into dancing and personal appearance again, and there was a fresh breeze of modernism, futuristic and exciting. Guys and girls were socializing together. MTV had just come out on the west coast, bringing a new wave of music, videos, bright colors, and a punch of stimulation. This "new wave" was a new start for us all, but especially me, and I was stoked.

I suppose a big part of my optimism came from meeting the new kids. I felt lucky to have crossed paths with them. I had been stuck in the land of grease and dudes and with the help of Alex found my way out. In one week everything had changed and the situation felt full of potential. Considering all the people I was meeting, I felt there was a good chance I could meet and get a girlfriend soon. I was a bit surprised that I was fitting in so well with them. I had always felt like such an outsider and was sure I would never fit into any halfway normal social group. I often hung out with the angry, hurt kids. These kids seemed to genuinely like me and I was going to roll with it.

A week later, Audrey's parents went out of town and she threw a party. Her family lived in a house in the hills above the Palisades with a spectacular view of the city. She put on Duran Duran's new four-song EP. This was before Rio came out. Hardly anybody in America knew who Duran Duran were at this point. This was new, cool music (yes, really). We cranked it up on her parent's fancy stereo and everyone danced like crazy. It was a clear night, the stars shone and the lights of the city were sparkling out the living room's sliding glass doors. Everyone was dancing enthusiastically, sweating, laughing and having a great time. It was innocent and sophisticated all at once.

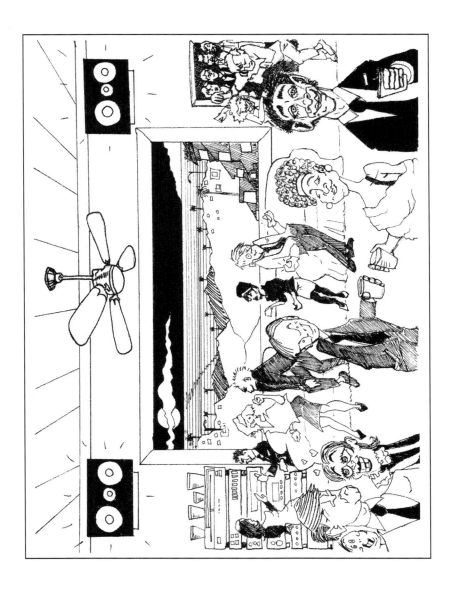

One Step Beyond

The funny thing was now I was more a part of Palisades High than when I had been a student there. I was hanging out at Pali during lunchtime on the days I didn't have classes at Santa Monica College and meeting new people there every day. One day Mr. Savich (my arresting principle) saw me and looked confused. He couldn't place me and probably figured that I was one of his students or he definitely would have kicked me out. Maybe it was my newly bleached white hair that threw him off.

On one of my visits, about a month into the school year, I was looking around Pali's outdoor quad and I realized that something was completely different from the year before but I couldn't pinpoint the change. It wasn't just the fashion; it had something to do with the way people were congregating. I pondered it for a while then realized that for the first time, a huge group of guys and girls were hanging out together. They began gathering on the outdoor stage, and new people added to the mix every day. This was not the case when I was in junior high at Paul Revere, or when I had been a student at Palisades High. We had always gathered in small cliques that were separated by gender with maybe 5 or 10 people at most. There had been a distinct hierarchy among these cliques and it was a given that the most popular was the volleyball team. Those guys had no doubt in their minds that they were the coolest. It was a given that the "volleyballers" had hung out in the same spot for the last 20 years. They were tan, smart, fit and girls loved them. And yes, most of them were jerks.

I imagined a horrifying conversation between a senior volleyball clique member taking his junior brother aside, arm around his shoulder, and pointing out to the quad.

Chad: "Chip?"

Chip, adoringly: "Yes, Chad?"

Chad: "Soon all of this will be yours. Respect the legacy."

Chip: "Gee ... Thanks, Chad," as Chip's eyes widen and a big tear drop falls onto his Topsider shoe.

All of the "lesser" cliques had a hard time putting together a decent social life for themselves. A lot of kids seemed a bit hopeless; they didn't bother to organize things for themselves. It seemed they didn't have the nerve, the guts or the energy. They would do their studying and wait for college, and with it, the hope of having fun.

Now it looked like the situation had changed over night. One of the changes came with the arrival of a group of mods from an alternative school in Santa Monica's Area D, which had closed down for some reason. These kids knew nothing of the social hierarchy that they were supposed to be oppressed by, and therefore hung out wherever and with whomever they chose. When they told me about their experience at Area D, I was confused, shocked and envious. They spoke of a small school, with small classes where they got individual attention from great teachers who were enthusiastic and supportive of the students.

"Huh? ... What?"

All of them, with just a few exceptions, got along well and were good friends with each other.

"Huh?"

And they called their teachers by their first names.

What?

I had never heard such a thing in my entire life! The teachers at Revere and Pali were underpaid, burned-out motherfuckers from the 50s or something. They were resentful and jealous of all the privileged little bastards and hated to bother having to educate them. Okay, to be fair, I had heard good things about two or three teachers who taught advanced placement classes, which, of course, I was never in. In all my years of formative education, I can remember two teachers I liked. Only two.

The alternative school sounded incredible. Where was I when they signed up for that shit? I didn't even know such a thing existed. When those kids came to Pali, most of them had healthy self-esteem and assumed it was normal to fit in well with others. They didn't see anything strange about having a lot of close friends. They revolutionized the social scene at Pali with their self-esteem and positivity.

Anybody with whom they came in contact could end up a potential friend. The group on the outdoor stage grew daily. It was never a clique; it began as Area D kids first, and then rapidly grew to include anyone. You could be a total dork, but if you were a decent person, you were in.

There was a mass exodus from the stuck-up, elitist, preppy cliques. They left by the dozens to join the outdoor stage, for this was where the action was. The once worshipped volleyball group was now boring and obsolete, sitting on the other side of the quad. Their scene just didn't have the appeal any longer.

I imagined Chad wailing: "This wasn't supposed to happen? I inherited this, like manifest destiny, from Chip, who said that I would now be the coolest, just like him."

Not anymore! Ha Ha!

The preppy look was looking stale and dying a painful death. New Wave and Mod had taken hold. The uniform had been this: Pink Ralph Lauren polo shirt (substitution, pink Izod Lacoste) wide wale corduroy pleated pants, Lacoste belt, and Topsider moccasins. The preppies were out of it now. Many of them ditched the clothes, cut their hair, and tried to squirm, apologize and wiggle their way across the lawn to the stage. The old regime was overthrown. I loved it and hoped it would last. There were parties every weekend with newly formed punk and mod bands. Smoking pot was over; burning out was done, for a while. You needed to be up on your feet for this music. This wasn't music you sat on the floor and listened to with headphones. I didn't want to be introspective and introverted anymore and stuck in my head. The early '80s seemed to be a reaction to the stagnation of the seventies, a reaction to the pot smoking and burning out to ridiculous overblown rock.

"Kansas, dude!"

"Boston ... dude!"

Anything that had the cheesy name of some city used to do just fine.

Not anymore. Now it was time to wash the haze out of the mind and dance and sweat. And it was a sweat that cleared the grime out of your head and soul.

Optimism! Fun, perhaps. I wanted out of my rut and it seemed others did too. I'm not saying that the '80s didn't have its problems: materialism, yuppification, crazed cocaine hoovering, greed, hedonism and basic assholism; but I'm just saying, that at the time, for a lot of people (including me!), it was a welcomed change.

One Step Beyond

***

I had just sold off my last metal shit heap. Now I just wanted one vehicle that ran. I bought a white Toyota four-wheel-drive long-bed truck. With that truck, I could go anywhere I wanted, and not worry about breaking down. I could put my surfboards in the back and drive along the ocean on the sand in Baja. I could sleep in the back. I could put friends in the back. I could put a girl in the back with me, if I could find one.

My current mission was to be social, meet more friends and girls, and, oh yeah, try to study.

One day, I hopped in my truck and drove to pick up my new friend, Randy, who was one of the Area D mod kids. We headed to a party at our friend Leslie's house; her parents were on vacation. We drove up the coast highway and took a right up Tuna Canyon, a narrow winding road up the mountains of Malibu. Her house was five miles up Tuna Canyon in a secluded area, which had incredible views of the mountains and ocean.

The plan was to meet six other kids at Leslie's and watch horror movies. We already started getting into a creepy mood while driving up the canyon road, which was dark and narrow with a few 180-degree turns, no guardrails and long drops to the bottom of the canyon. The people who live there had a lot of nerve because, if the canyon wasn't on fire, it was flooding. The routine is burn in October, then flood during the winter. Fires happen every few years in Malibu. They get whipped up around the end of summer, during the hot, dry, offshore Santa Ana wind conditions.

Randy and I had the Psychedelic Furs Love My Way cranked up and we were singing along when we came around a turn and suddenly were alarmed to find a homeless man standing in the middle of the road, 30 yards or so in front of us, with his arms outstretched. He was staring up into space, shaking in convulsions. He appeared to be having some kind of cosmic spasms. I braked and swerved around him.

"What the fuck!" I said.

"Whoa!" said Randy.

"That was crazy!"

He had long hair, a beard, and he was filthy, with tattered clothes. He faced us directly, standing in the middle of our lane, having his seizure, reaching out, like Jesus, to the sky. It was insane. I had no idea what it meant, but it seemed like some kind of a sign, a sign I didn't bother to interpret. Maybe it had something to do with aliens, or God, perhaps? It probably had more to do with schizophrenia. It reminded me of another disturbing canyon incident that I experienced a couple years earlier.

My old motorcycle friend Steve and I were hiking at night up Temescal Canyon when we heard a bunch of people chanting up ahead of us on the trail. Steve wanted to keep going up the canyon and check it out. I told him, hell no, that we were close enough. We were about a hundred feet away. The cult members were on both sides of the canyon across from each other and they were taking turns chanting and mumbling back and forth, like call and response. We listened to them for a couple minutes and I was terrified. We realized that they were also communicating with each other by making clicking sounds with their tongues. I wanted to flee, quickly and quietly, but Steve began walking further up the canyon. He was only about fifty feet away from them now. I was twenty feet back. I could hear his feet making little snapping sounds as he walked over twigs and stones. All of a sudden the chanting and mumbling and clicking stopped. There was silence. They had heard us? Steve and I stopped and were perfectly still, hoping not to be detected. I thought we were going to be sacrificially murdered and never heard from again. I turned and ran the hell out of there as fast as I could. Then Steve started running so fast that he flew right by me. It felt like I was a disembodied head flying down the canyon in the dark. I wasn't thinking about where to step, just flying like a low aircraft, stoned as hell, scared out of my mind. We ran out from the canyon trailhead into the parking lot. We saw two other vehicles, white vans, parked beside my car. They had spooky, hieroglyphic-like symbols on the side.

They might have been harmless; they might have been straight from hell. But I'm glad we didn't stick around to find out.

We arrived at Leslie's house, had a few beers and socialized with everyone for a couple of hours and started watching part of American Werewolf in London on video. Then Randy and I got fidgety and decided to go off-roading.

Tuna Canyon had acres and acres of open land on the top of a cliff that overlooked the ocean at one end. The rolling hills were covered with eucalyptus. It was a great place to go for walks or drive off-road vehicles. There were a lot of trails to venture down, and some muddy ponds. There had been some days of heavy rain; the winter of '82 was already proving to be a wet one. Some years, it only rains once or twice in southern California.

We were all dressed up, darting around in my truck on the top of the dark mountain. I was wearing a white dress shirt and grey wool pants. Randy was in an all white "eighties" puffy outfit that most likely included shoulder pads.

We got stuck in a small lake that night. We were driving along and I saw a big section of water in front of me.

I said to Randy, "I wonder how deep that is?"

I quickly found the answer, too deep.

I sat there for a while, considering going through it (when I simply could've gone around it). Randy said, "That's not deep. It's probably about a foot."

I figured (sure) we should try to go through it instead of simply around it. We got about halfway through and my wheels started spinning and we bogged down into the mud. My truck wasn't going anywhere so I took my foot off the accelerator and put it in neutral. I stared at my friend, perplexed. It was dark, and eerie outside and we were sitting in my truck at midnight in the middle of a small lake, all dressed up, with water about up to the bottom of the door. Randy elected to get out and start wading around, assessing the situation.

Okay. The exhaust pipe was under water. Bubbling. The water was up to his hips, three and a half feet deep; his previously pure white, puffy clothes were now chocolaty brown. I looked out the window and saw him lean down with his face to the surface of the water, scooping mud out from underneath the tires in an attempt to get them to touch firm ground. He was scraping out the goop with his bare hands. I sat, clean inside my truck, watching all this like it was on TV.

I yelled orders out the window: "Randy, push the truck from the back!" He pushed it as hard as he could while I gunned the engine. It was no use. Maybe I could back out?

He went to the front of the truck, leaned forward and started pushing the hood. I hit the gas and water forcefully blasted all over him, most of it shooting in his face. He was still pushing, though. I gave him credit for that. None of that worked so I got out of the truck and lowered myself into the water to join him. We both worked at digging underneath the tires. We finally hit semi-packed earth. After about a half hour of digging, we got enough traction and escaped. We returned to the party, muddy from head to toe. Everyone laughed at us for about fifteen minutes straight. Leslie took our clothes and put them in the washer. We all jumped into the Jacuzzi in our underwear. We listened to the Specials, drinking beer, talking about music, under the stars, looking out over the ocean. Getting stuck in a pond didn't matter; I wasn't embarrassed. I was just happy we got out. I was enjoying my new friends and was the happiest I had ever been. It wouldn't be long, though, before I'd gravitate back, unconsciously, toward the angry kids, the punkers, and the mentally disturbed. Underneath my newly found confidence and feeling of hope, I was still a young, hurt and angry guy with low self-esteem and a powerful pull toward frustration and loneliness.

Mike Pearson

One Step Beyond

Meet The Blaines
"Kids of the Black Hole" by Adolescents

The first time I encountered the Blaines I was at a Pali High swim-team party. They were getting thrown out.

What's a Blaine?

They were two short, bald, identical twin, punk rock brothers. They were also known as the Insanes. It was the beginning of October and I went with Randy to a swim team party at a house on Friends Street (Randy was on the swim team). We drove past our elementary school and a couple of churches, and took a right on Friends. This was the perfect American neighborhood. White picket fences, manicured lawns, gardens, and fresh paint jobs. I always had the feeling something sinister might have been going on under these gabled roofs. On the surface the neighborhood was ideal, with wonderful, clean, (happy?) people. The only thing wrong with this dream, the only thing that indicated that something might be wrong in Happyland, was the looming presence of a giant, obnoxious, rectangular, white stucco box of a house. This abomination was three times as large as any other house in the neighborhood. It had a ten-foot-wide stripe of shiny, blue tile around it. This home wasn't doing "quaint" like the rest of them. It was belligerent. It looked like a ship. I had gone to a couple of parties there while in junior high and knew the girl, Kathleen, who lived there. Her dad made money in an unmentionable way: Porno!

In a way, I had respect for that house and its nerve. Its attitude was, "Fuck You." The neighbors hated it so much they petitioned the city to have it torn down; they argued that it wasn't built to code. Eventually they were successful.

Kathleen lived there with her little brother and dad. Her mom had left the family years ago. Kathleen was a gorgeous, blonde, ninth-grade, coke-snorting party girl and she lived in the guesthouse in back. Kids partied in the large kidney-shaped Jacuzzi, which ran halfway underneath the main house. The dad designed the house but he had never finished it. There was no grass in front, just large mounds of dirt and weeds with construction debris. The father was arrested a few years later and the house was torn down to the neighbors' delight.

In an acceptable house on Friends street, the swim team party was going strong. The Blaines had crashed the party and I arrived right when they were being thrown out.

I saw Rick Blaine struggling, thrashing, and twisting about as he was lifted and hauled through the front entryway by a muscular swim-team hunk. Rick's crime was that he and his friends had taken off the New Wave music (Haircut 100) and put on the Dead Kennedys and were slam dancing furiously in the living room. Rick Blaine was a wiry, 5 foot 7 inch tall, punk rocker with buzzed, quarter-inch, dyed black hair. He looked a lot like a young Johnnie Rotten. He was wearing his usual outfit: an old black ripped punk t-shirt (with the name and logo of a punk band—Void), ripped jeans with the names of punk bands that he drew on them with permanent markers, and tall black Doc Martin boots that went way up his ankles, topped off with spiked wrist bracelets and a nose ring.

His brother, Tim, was hanging out in the street with some other punks, sitting on the hood of an old car. Tim was dressed identically to Rick, except he had a bleached white buzz-cut and a little less writing on his clothes. It would be hard to tell them apart if their hair hadn't been different colors. The swim-team guy hated the fact that Rick was slam dancing in his mother's living room, so he grabbed him and personally threw him out the front door, slamming his black fuzzy head into the doorjamb on the way.

Rick was pissed! Tim and the other punks were pissed too! The swim team guys were skinheads, as well, so this was just a big, angry, bald scene. Everyone yelled at one another for a few minutes but it never escalated into a fight. The Blaines and the punks basically backed down. They knew they would get their asses kicked by the swim team. Rick spent the rest of the night pacing around outside, ranting and raving to his brother and their group of younger followers about the disrespect.

He screamed empty threats for two hours to an increasingly bored and tired crowd of partiers. He bellowed about how they were going to get Suicidal Tendencies (the most psycho punk band around) to kill them.

I thought the ranting and raving was funny. I hung out and listened for about an hour to Rick's insane diatribe about how lame the fucking swim team was, and how lame their party was, and how they were going to be "dead!"

"You pussies! Try to swim your way out of this one! You guys are so dead! When the Suicidals find out about this, they're going to have fun pissing all over your mom's Indian rug. Fu-uck You!"

I liked these guys. I liked their anger. I was resonating with their anger, and their anger gave me the sense of freedom to feel my own anger. My rage had been stuffed inside for so many years. I had always been so "nice," and had suppressed so much emotion that I had long ago become depressed.

A few days later I ran into them again as I walked out of the back of Mort's Deli (a local hangout). They were sitting on the sidewalk folding newspapers. This was what they did every day at 3 p.m. They were paperboys and The Evening Outlook was their paper.

They would fold the papers, and wrap them with a rubber band, then ride off on dirt bikes to do their routes. They were the oldest paperboys ever, eleventh graders. Their dad was the guy who dropped off all the papers at 3 a.m. He was also an algebra teacher at the community college and wanted the twins to keep delivering, even though they were old.

My mod friends already knew the Blaines; the Blaines had been delivering papers to their houses since elementary school. The mods and the Blaines hadn't yet had a serious disagreement stemming from their opposing ideologies. The punks and mods had been pretty cordial with each other...Until today. Today the Blaines were pissed off at the mods!

Rick and Tim were ranting and raving while sitting and folding papers. A couple of their followers were pissed off, too, standing by, arms crossed. The night before, some mods had spray-painted a little skanking man (a mod icon) on the Blaines' sidewalk, where they folded papers every day. It was a deliberate gesture of disrespect intended to humiliate and provoke them. And it worked.

I stood there listening to their grievances when the mods came out of the back door of Mort's. The mods walked up and stood there silently. Rick Blaine looked up at Randy and his crew. He started laughing nervously and shaking his head back and forth. Then he tried to bring up the subject in a non-accusatory way.

"Very funny. Very, very funny. That's a good one. A little funky, dancing fag!"

Randy and the mods listened for a while to the Blaines' deep concern and hard feelings about the incident. The mods remained quiet and did not confess to painting it there the night before. They just listened. Then came the accusation and the finger pointing.

"Fuck!" Rick said, "Which one of you assholes painted this skank'n dick on my sidewalk?"

Calmly, Randy said, "Don't know? But it looks pretty good. Don't you think, Rupert?" to his brother. They looked at each other and smiled.

"If I found out you guys did it, you're fucking so dead."

"What are you going to do?" Randy replied. "Throw a newspaper through our window?" The mod brothers smiled at each other again uncomfortably.

Rick started laughing, maniacally, like a hyena, bouncing up and down.

"That's not a bad idea," Rick said, while heaving and hawing.

Rupert said, "We gotta do homework," and they left.

I decided to stay and talk to the Blaines about punk rock and find out what bands they liked and what shows they'd seen. Rick launched into some punk rock stories about how somebody pounded somebody's head in at this show and did a back flip and landed on a piece of wood that was sticking up, and got a bottle smashed over their head while diving off a twenty-foot-high P.A. speaker and snapped his spinal column into several pieces and how it was just "hilarious" and they couldn't stop laughing about it afterwards.

I told them how I was really into punk and went to a lot of shows with my friend, Pinsky from Santa Monica back in the ninth grade in '79. They were obviously in awe of me, so I kept on bragging about the great punk shows I had seen, and they missed. I went on about Fear, X, The Crowd, The Weirdos, The Dickies, Black Flag, Germs, Circle Jerks, Flipper, Adolescents, Dead Kennedys, Geza X and the Mommymen, Suburban Lawns, The Plugz, etc.

The Blaines were the first people I had met from the Palisades who shared my love of punk rock. Most people just thought punk was stupid, melody-less and noisy. I felt they were too stupid to understand how great it was.

I hadn't really been into punk for the last two years and I had lost touch with Pinsky on purpose. I had been in too many dangerous situations with that kid. I felt way out of control when I hung out with him. Like I might die. We were fourteen years old, stoned, and riding my moped sometimes twenty or thirty miles to punk shows, often out until 3 and 4 in the morning on school nights! Neither one of us had any parental supervision, guidance, or limits set. We drank and smoked weed and popped pills. We even took PCP and LSD a few times, which I think tweaked my brain and psyche way for the worse. I took everything except for heroin. He had just started messing with that when I decided to distance myself from him. Pinsky and I always ended up in crazy situations: Since when do you ride a moped on the freeway?! He was getting crazier and crazier, taking drugs daily, having unprotected sex with wild old (twenty-something) punk women in their beat up old cars.

When I brought up Pinsky the Blaines said, "No way!" (Pinsky was legendary to them.) They had seen him at shows and knew that he hung out with members of various L.A. punk bands, like The Germs and Black Flag and with the infamous Dogtown vertical skateboarding pioneers, Tony Alva and Jay Adams.

Pinsky was a small ratty-looking kid who reminded me of Ratso Rizzo from Midnight Cowboy. In '79 he had quarter-inch-long, white-bleached hair, with a four-inch-wide black-died stripe running along one side. It's hard to explain how radical a hair-do like that was back then. It was simply out of the question for everyone but maybe .000002 percent of the population. I'm guessing only about a hundred people in the U.S. looked anything like that back then. Nowadays, of course you can see those hairstyles on TV and in any mall—and it's adorable!

I told the Blaines that Pinsky and I got into punk from listening to Rodney On The Roq on KROQ and reading the L.A. Weekly. KROQ was only in L.A. and had such a small signal you couldn't hear it everywhere. We spent a lot of our post 9th grade summer in his house smoking pot, drinking and listening to punk and new wave. We always had his house to ourselves. He was the ultimate latchkey kid. His mom was a stewardess, and we only saw her about once a week. His dad left when he was two.

That summer Pinsky met a strange, sketchy, middle-aged man who put us to work selling bootleg t-shirts and scalping tickets outside concert halls and arenas. We would stand on backed-up freeway off-ramps selling the t-shirts out of backpacks to people who were getting wasted in their cars while waiting to park for the concert. We would spend the night at the Coliseum and the Sports Arena doing drugs, hanging out with homeless hustlers, vagrants, prostitutes, and more the well-to-do scalpers after selling t-shirts at the rock shows.

We also would wait in ticket lines over and over again buying as many tickets as we could to giant concerts like Elton John. That was when it took big shows a few hours to sell out because it wasn't computerized through Ticketmaster; it was just sold through the venue. I totally impressed the

Blaines with stories of smoking sherms (angel-dust laced Sherman cigarettes) with the sketchy ticket scalpers.

"No way!" Rick said. "You did PCP?" He thought that was so cool. "That's elephant tranquilizer, man!" He started to laugh, hyena-style, with his shoulders pulsing up and down. Tim asked me: "What was it like? I heard that shit is bad news!"

"It made me feel like my head was disconnected from my body," I said.

Then I told them about how in the eighth grade, before conversion to punk rock, we went to the two day California World Music Festival at the Coliseum and saw Ted Nugent, Cheap Trick, Van Halen, Aerosmith, Molly Hatchet, April Wine, Boomtown Rats, Eddie Money, The Outlaws, UFO and Toto, etc. I made sure not to include that we actually liked those bands and had a great time! I also did not include that Cheap Trick was my favorite, and how I had a peak experience on acid as they played while the sun set with these unbelievable shades of red and blue in sky behind them as the wind blew through their voluminous rock star hair. Live at Budokan had come out that year and they were superstars. There were about 80,000 people there each day to see the bands. I remember moving through the massive crowd, enjoying myself beyond belief, fourteen and frying, moving like a amoeba through the thousands of people, with no effort, getting squished, but it never being painful. I was one with all the people and everything in the universe. I remembered having the realization that all I had to do to move to the front quickly was just get the very tip of my shoulder in front of someone else's shoulder then I would automatically pop in front of them. All the pressure from behind would pop me forward without effort. I remember just flowing through the thousands of people, going wherever I wanted with great ease.

Then the Blaines shared some of their punk stories. I had loved punk rock and was so excited to find other enthusiastically pissed off people from my town who enjoyed it too.

I knew there was a tendency to stretch the truth when it came to punk-rock battle stories, but I actually believed the Blaines when they lowered their voices, looking around to make sure nobody was listening, and began to tell me about the latest incident involving a famous sitcom actor who lived in the Palisades. "We couldn't believe it." Rick said, shaking his head. "Fred Price was driving by in his big old' Cadillac. I just stood up 'cause I got through folding, and I look in, and I see Fred Price, and I get a glimpse of all these dildos and vibrators and stuff sitting on the passenger seat, and I couldn't believe it! I go, "Tim, get up, quick, look!" Rick handed the story off to Tim.

"And I couldn't believe it, dude," Tim said. "There, on his seat, were all these dildos and stuff like that, and we're like, no way… you fucking pervert! He sees us looking in, and he reaches over quickly and covers it all up with a pink sweater or something. We yelled asinine comments as he drove away, "Aaagh—Fred Price! You fucking Pervert! You fucking Sicko!" They were so committed to the story. I wasn't used to people being such liars, for fun. They squinted their eyes at the same time, shook their heads back and forth slowly, and said earnestly: "I swear to God, dude." The next day I saw them again in town and they started laughing their heads off. "You believed us? Fred Price's got dildos on his seat? JESUS!" After that, I knew to throw out at least half of whatever they said.

The twins were so much alike—angry, oppositional-defiant and punk—but they always insisted that they were nothing like each other. Each of them said that they couldn't stand the other one. And they always had to have opposite hair. Rick black, Tim white. Or Tim black and Rick white. They also had separate friends. At first, I thought I could be friends with both of them, but that didn't work. They were too jealous of each other. So I ended up being friends with Tim.

Most people thought the Blaines were total rebels. In a lot of ways they were. They did destroy practically anything they got their hands on. Party dismantling was their specialty. But these rebels were not totally rebellious. They were from a devout Catholic family and they attended mass every day at five o'clock. These rebels had each been "Alter Boy Of The Year" at one point. Contrary to their intolerance, hostility, and nihilistic rage, they proclaimed a deep dedication to their Lord Jesus Christ.

The Blaines sure did believe in their church and God! If you said you didn't, watch out, they might threaten to pull out a gun and blow your fuckin' head off! They were right-wing extremists in all areas. They were tough on crime (unless it was their own crimes). They loved capital punishment. They loved guns. And they hated bleeding-heart liberals and "hand-outs." They hated pot and hippies with a passion. They said that hippies were pathetic, unrealistic losers living in Fantasyland. They often used the word "realists" to describe themselves. I personally found these "realists" to be the most pessimistic people I'd ever met.

It was pretty obvious that a good amount of their anger came not from "Society," but from not getting any approval, love or acknowledgment from their father, Gunther. Gunther was old, angry and brittle. He rarely spoke. He just sat in his big Barcalounger swivel chair. Gunther never once said hi to me any of the countless times I entered his house. They lived in a post-war tract house. Gunther was sitting right there in the living room reading the paper as I came in the front door and would never say anything, no acknowledgment. My dad sat in his big chair, too, quiet and withdrawn, as well, reading his paper or watching TV, but at least there was a gentleness and caring somewhere under his disengaged self. I figured at least my dad wasn't constantly disapproving and sending out disgusted vibes like Gunther. Gunther was the most disgruntled person I had ever met.

Tim seemed to have given up trying with his father. Rick still seemed to be working on trying to get a little approval by doing well in school. Gunther was a math professor and he valued education. Rick studied hard and brought home all A's in math and science. His grades were funny, though; they were always something like A, U, U, and "U" was "unsatisfactory." The two categories, I think, were "work habits" and "cooperation."

Gunther probably cared about his sons on some level, but there wouldn't be a chance in hell he would ever show it. My dad was not affectionate or demonstrative in any of those ways either, but he could sometimes (a couple times a year) squeak out, "Love you, Bruthy," after I would say, "Love you, dad," first. Bruthy was short for "brother." Gunther made my dad look like Mike Brady. I never even heard Gunther say a word to them. I did hear him grunt a couple times as they walked by. The brothers said that he would often just insult them. That was as much as they might expect from Gunther. He would tell them that they were worthless losers. Maybe if they weren't punk "losers" they might not even get that from him.

I tried taking Gunther's algebra class at Santa Monica College, but he taught too fast and I was too scared to ask questions so I dropped it. The Blaines' mom seemed kind and loving, though. She was like my mom in the way that she burdened and impinged on her sons by reaching out to them to get some of her emotional needs met since her husband didn't want anything to do with her. Their family had the same dynamic as mine. Dad was disengaged—from everyone. The brothers didn't get along. The mom was needy, clingy and talked incessantly and had that incongruent positive "happy" attitude all the time. The similar crazy family dynamic might have been one reason why the Blaines and I were drawn to each other. We resonated on a weird subconscious level. We were hurt, confused, angry and frustrated and wanted to wear it on our sleeves. At times I would still hang out with the healthier crowd (the mods), but the pull of the Blaines was strong. After a week or two we formed a punk band and I was spending most of my time with Tim and his friends.

One Step Beyond

Violent Attack II, Too
"Wild in the Streets" by Circle Jerks

On Friday night Tim Blaine and I headed over to his friend's house, Mike Johnson's, to play some punk rock in his garage. Johnson was also known as Mr. Insane. Mr. Insane was going to sing—or yell, to be more exact. I was going to play bass, and my friend Ian would play drums. Tim was rocking out, playing loud, distorted guitar, as I entered the garage. He reminded me of a cross between a punk William Shatner (same body style and movements, similar face) and Frankenstein, as he moved about the garage on a sonic rampage. Johnson was sitting on an amplifier, nodding his head to the music, drinking a forty-ounce beer. Johnson was tall, 6'4," with a strong, cut, body and a dark blonde, buzz cut. He had been on the swim team last year. His personality alternated between quiet and shy and completely intense and crazy. Intense and crazy happened when he drank.

Ian set his kick-drum in place while Tim and Johnson eyed him suspiciously. It was true: Ian looked New Wave, Ian was New Wave. He had a lot of hair on the top, curly, puffed up and "New Romantic." I thought Ian was a great guy. He was open-minded, loved all kinds of music; he was an interesting guy. He was one of the Area D kids. I was hoping that the Blaines would accept him, but I wasn't expecting that to happen. Truth be told, he wasn't very good on drums. He never practiced, but I thought he almost made up for it with his enthusiasm.

By 7 p.m. we had everything set up and we started to jam. Five neighborhood kids wandered in and started drinking beer and listening. Some of them sang along and sat in on instruments on songs they knew. We had the best time ever! We played like escaped mental patients that night. Noisy and crazy.

We played some D.O.A. songs, some Black Flag songs, some punk versions of The Who songs, like I'm Free, and a bunch of Tim's original songs.

One Step Beyond

I thought Johnson was an awesome and great singer. It was weird the way he would scream the songs while stalking maniacally around the garage, and then a few moments later he would be sitting there quietly, shy and introverted. After jamming for about three sweaty hours we put our instruments down and opened the garage door and went out to the driveway to get some fresh air. We talked about how rad it sounded and that we should make it a real band.

A few moments later a Mercedes sedan rolled up to the curb. It stopped at the house next door. We saw both right side doors open. Three severely inebriated punk rockers were tossed out of the car, and they landed in the gutter. We couldn't see who threw them out. The Mercedes peeled away. "That's Rick!" Tim shouted, as he raced over to them. We all went over there and shook our heads in disbelief as we stood over the wasted punkers. They had make-up smeared grotesquely all over their faces, their clothes were ripped and torn and tied in funny ways (they looked like they were wearing punk rock halter tops). Rick's forehead said "Asshole" on it, written in lipstick.

Rick and another kid were passed out. The other one was fading in and out of consciousness. We dragged them into the garage and continued to jam on music for another hour. The music we made was like a surrealistic soundtrack to their plight.

The next day at the Blaines' house, Rick told us what had happened. He was in bad shape, recovering from his worst hangover ever. "Oh, man," he said. "We went over to this chick's house—me and Timmy and those guys—and we started partying hard. We raided the liquor cabinet, then we put on the Sex Pistols, and we were jumping up and down, slamming, thrashing, on this chick's bed (the full little girl bed). We fucked up the springs, dude!" He started the hyena laugh, his shoulders started going up and down, then it reverberated into his splitting head and he had to stop laughing. "Oh, man, I drank like a half a big bottle of Jack, and Timmy drank almost a whole bottle of Southern Comfort, and since he only weighs like seventy-five pounds, he blew chunks everywhere, all over this chick's mansion." It looked like it was making him sick to talk about it. "Then I guess we started going crazy in the house. I can't remember. But I think that's what happened. That was the last thing I remember."

"So they tied you up and painted you with makeup?" I said. "Because when I saw you, you had been tossed out of a car and you had 'Asshole' written on your forehead."

"I guess so. Those fucking bitches." He laughed a little. That night was the beginning of our band Violent Attack 2. We used to like to think of our band as Violent Attack #1, though. Brief band history: Tim used to play in Violent Attack with his brother on bass, but they didn't get along. They argued constantly then they split up. Rick formed his own band and took the name with him. But Tim wanted the name, too. Now there were twin bands for twin brothers. The truth was that we were Violent Attack #2, because Rick was using the band name first.

Rick's Violent Attack was actually pretty great. They had Timmy, a little fifteen-year-old bleach-blonde kid on guitar. He was talented and intense. They had a famous singer-songwriter's son on drums. That kid was good, he'd been playing since he was very young. Their songs were mostly originals, written by Rick. Tim said they sucked shit, but they were good. I felt we had catchier songs, though, and you couldn't ask for a more insane singer than Johnson. That was of utmost importance: a great punk singer should either be crazy or truly seem it. Violent Attack 2 played for a month with Ian on drums. Then we got a new drummer because Tim said Ian just wasn't cutting it. He was right, Ian was sloppy and had bad timing. He just hadn't put enough time behind the drums. Tim recruited his old friend, Adam, from San Gabriel. Adam was a member of the first Violent Attack and he was an awesome drummer. He pounded the drums intensely with great force, but perfectly on time. Tim always talked about how lucky we were to have Adam because he "wailed just like Chuck Biscuits," one of punk's great drummers. Every Friday afternoon, Johnson, Tim and I drove in my truck to Adam's house in San Gabriel to practice. We would rehearse in his garage for about five or six hours. His parents were really nice. They were old-fashioned 1950s-style parents. They dressed 50s and even had a 1950s ranch house. They weren't trying to be retro or anything; they just never changed with the times. His parents never complained about the noise, and neither did the neighbors. I didn't take that for granted. San Gabriel was so different from the Palisades. We were never able to practice in the Palisades. The town was too loaded with crabby, rich, anal white people who had no tolerance for kids or noise. The closest thing to being able to practice in the Palisades was when you just plugged in your instrument and it made that humming-buzzing sound. By then the cops were at your door telling you not to even hit a single note or they'd take your instruments. We rehearsed steadily at Adam's house, and within two months we had a 25 song set. Fifteen covers and ten originals. Short songs, about two and half minutes each.

One Step Beyond

That winter we played Palisades parties almost every weekend. We played a lot of parties we weren't even invited to. We would find out about a party and we'd just show up with all our equipment and plug in and start playing. It was funny because no one ever told us that we couldn't play. People didn't want to get the Blaines pissed off at them so they would just go along with it. The fear wasn't so much getting beat up. It was that the Blaines would never stop giving a person shit for a slight. They had a knack for talking shit to people about some past impropriety and never stopping.

"You pussy, man. You wimped out, not letting us play your party. You could've been the most popular person in the school if we had played. People would've thought you were so cool—and you know that's all you care about anyway, you conformist society tool. You blew it! You're party would've fucking rocked, but instead you were just sticking tea and crumpets up each other's asses." They'd go on and on.

A lot of kids from the Palisades had mixed feelings about the Blaines. The Blaines caused a lot of trouble, and some kids despised them for their destructive nature and abuse. But the Blaines also brought a lot of fun and excitement wherever they went. Many kids respected their defiance. Many kids from the Palisades were angry but were unable to rebel; they found themselves having to appreciate the BMW and the paid vacation to the college of their parents' dream. The Blaines felt and expressed anger for a lot of the "good" kids of the community. It was like a public service and provided a vicarious rush. Kids appreciated them for that.

Also, a lot of kids really liked Violent Attack's aggressive music. It was a release, and something kind of cool, creative and modern. Most girls just thought it was a screaming mess of noise, but it wasn't just noise. It was artistic noise! A wailing wall of power chords with heavy feedback, manic grumbling and rumbling bass, and angry, bombastic drums with psychotic, ranting vocals. What more could a teen dude ask for?

When we weren't practicing, I spent most of my time at the Blaines' house listening to punk, playing with their pet snakes and cutting and dying hair. Haircuts were an important matter. The Blaines would only allow their hair to grow out to about an inch before it was too long and they would buzz it again. If hair grew out to an inch you were a hippie and you didn't want to be that. Their mom had us do our haircuts in the front driveway with an extension cord on the buzzer because she was sick of all the hair in the house from the constant haircuts. One of the Blaine tests of how punk you were was what level electric shaver you had the nerve for because crew cuts were still uncommon then.

They insisted you have a buzz cut if you wanted to hang with them. To them, a Level Four haircut was the wimpiest. It allowed for the longest possible hair length—about a half-inch. The Blaines prided themselves on Level One, which left you with an eighth inch of hair. Most kids would go for Level Three; that meant they didn't have to be bald (and mom wouldn't get too upset), and the Blaines wouldn't label them as total wimps either.

Tim might say, "You're totally wimping. But that's okay, you fucking hippie," then he would switch the cutter to Level One anyway and start buzzing.

One Step Beyond

I had the pleasure of giving one kid, who we called Chunky Monkey, a double-mohawk. He looked really awful with that haircut, a bald 15-year-old with two bizarre, naturally bright red stripes running down both sides of his head. The Blaines gave him the name Chunky Monkey a few months earlier when he blew chunks, while looking like an orangutan with his wild red hair, at a punk show after consuming too many Lucky Lagers.

Tim and Rick and I bleached our hair white. We had been doing my hair white for a couple months, so we were professionals and knew how to get past the orange stage. Tim figured we'd bleach five times in a row with the strongest peroxide. Then we'd add this powder called "Lightening Booster Reactor," which always fried our hair to the maximum, but it took all the yellow and orange out.

Rick wanted me to paint a thin black stripe of the blackest black around Rick's newly bleached-white head. I knew it would look ridiculous, but I also knew he would probably be the only one in America with a hairstyle like it. So I started making the stripe on his head with my black-dyed finger. As I went along, I realized I was creating a horseshoe-shaped stripe, about 3/4 inch thick, which stretched from one temple to the other curving around the back of his crown.

Needless to say, it took balls to walk out of the house with that hairdo. Over the next few days, Rick had gotten so many comments about how bad it looked that he couldn't take it anymore and shaved his head bald. As he shaved his head, he couldn't stop there, though. If he was going to get rid of the horseshoe, he needed to replace it with something equally heinous, so no one could accuse him of "wimping." So he shaved his eyebrows off.

He looked real bad. People were confused when they saw him, because he didn't really look human. He looked like he was from outer space. He was always an outcast, but now he had taken it to another level, and we commended him for it.

Kids from the neighborhood got caught up in all the excitement the Blaines and their bands brought on. A lot of guys and girls were turning punk at this time.

We had a friend, Sean, who was a good example of the new popularity of punk. He had suddenly turned punk a couple months earlier. The Blaines taunted him endlessly about his recent switch from his former nerdy existence. They made fun of his Doc Martin boots that were too new looking (even though he tried to scuff them up the best he could).

Sean couldn't fool us; we all remembered him from when he was a "normal guy" a few weeks ago. He was a big, tall seventeen-year-old, who lumbered around off-balance. Superficially he seemed tough, because he was big and had a shaved head, big black boots, torn jeans, and a crass t-shirt (same "hardcore" outfit as the Blaines, basically), but underneath it all he was studious, polite and a good kid.

One night at one of the parties he got together with a young punk girl.

He was drunk; she was drunk. They were punk!

He knew that she was on the young side, but he decided not to acknowledge that. She was very cute and had spiky, bleached hair, with at least a dozen earrings. She was kind of a tough, too—that is, for a girl of the Westside.

After school one day the Blaines decided to rub it in real hard, making a big point of what age she actually was.

Tim said: "She's thirteen, dude!"

"Oh, no ... Oh, man. You've got to be kidding," Sean said, alarmed, though he knew damn well how old she was.

"She's thirteen!" Tim said it again.

"Oh, man." Sean said, still shaking his head, and looking at the ground. "I didn't know that," as if it were the major mistake of his life.

It went on like that for weeks, but on the weekends, when there were parties, we'd always see him with her again, kissing and making out. That went on for a month or so. Then she decided to break up with him, because he was too obsessed and she was only thirteen and didn't want to deal with that.

The Blaines couldn't stop bagging on him for falling for her. They were probably jealous because they never had girlfriends. And they loved to taunt him. They weren't morally concerned about her age ... what did they care?

Whenever our band played a party, and Sean was there, we'd always be sure to include in our set a song by D.O.A. called "13." Before launching into it, Tim would yell into the microphone: "This one's for Sean, the fuckin' Pervert!" Or another time he might yell: "This one's for our friend, the Child Molester!"

Johnson would shout the words:

"She's only 13! And I'm one Big Zero!

She's only 13! And that's just right for me!

'Cause I'm one big zero...and she's only 13..."

Sean would try really hard not to show how pissed he was. He would just walk away from watching the band and then he'd end up screaming at a wall and kicking a trashcan or something.

The next day the Blaines would try again to push him to the brink when they'd ask him all casually, "Hey Sean, did you hear us play '13' last night?"

He'd plaster a smile across his face and say, "No, I didn't hear it," and then he'd walk away, super mad, kicking something. We would laugh and laugh, because asking him if he heard it was ridiculous—we made it a point to play it at least three times a party.

Sean took a lot of shit from the Blaines in order to be friends with them. They could be incredibly mean. So far they had been respectful to me (to my face, at least), so I didn't have a problem with them, yet.

Most kids from the Palisades did have a problem with them. The Blaines would crash every party, get really drunk and end up breaking things and insult people brutally and make girls cry. The Blaines would thrash the house and scare girls off the dance floor. There were keg parties nearly every weekend and kids would get super drunk, but the drunkest people were always the Blaines.

One Friday night a couple of really nice sisters threw a party, and their mom was there, and she was the sweetest mom in the world, and the party was pretty mellow. Tim was upstairs and instead of walking down the stairs, he went commando over the banister down the living room wall and left these really awful black boot marks on the white wall. People just shook their heads, horrified.

One Step Beyond

Somehow I got away with not being lumped in as one of them, one of "the Blaines," even though I was in the band and hung out with them all the time. I guess it was because I was nice to most people and refrained from wrecking things.

Tim and Rick weren't the only ones causing the problems. Destruction was always accomplished with the help of Mr. Insane. Before a party was over, Tim and Johnson had to do something they thought was real funny, like throwing someone's lawn furniture off the cliff. Liquor was always the main contributing factor. As time went on, Johnson was acting more psychotic due to alcohol abuse and who knows … mental illness? After awhile pretty much every time he drank he would get hammered beyond belief, lose control and go ballistic, and then black out. When he wasn't drinking he was a really nice guy.

I first met Johnson at Paul Revere Junior High. I remembered him as being quiet, introverted and strange, but seemingly civilized. That was during eighth grade, 1978, when he sat next to me in Youth and Law. Youth and Law was the only class I liked besides wood shop. We talked about the Jim Jones Guyana tragedy that had just happened. I was intrigued by the story. (Jim Jones was a charming guy who got a whole bunch of people together to form a cult and they drank cyanide-flavored Kool Aid and died.) We also discussed another weird event: San Francisco city supervisor Dan White shot and killed Mayor George Moscone and supervisor and gay rights activist Harvey Milk, and White served only six years for manslaughter because the jury felt sorry for him because they found that he was under the influence of Twinkies. Yes, Twinkies. I thought that story was insane.

Johnson also intrigued me, he always wore this mysterious Talking Heads T-shirt, and he rarely spoke. The Talking Heads? What? What is that? How could there be a band in existence with that odd of a name? I thought it was just very bizarre. I didn't know anything about punk or new wave at this point. I hadn't even heard of this "new music." Before 1978, my friends and I only knew of classic rock bands. Led Zeppelin, Pink Floyd, Aerosmith, Lynyrd Skynyrd and so on. What was up with this guy, Johnson? How did he know of such a band? Who turned him on to it? (He found out about it from his older sister.)

Besides the weird-ass Talking Heads T-shirt, as far as I could tell Johnson seemed shy but not too freakish. Later that year, though, he fell out of a fifteen-foot-high tree house, while on acid, and crashed through a greenhouse, and slammed his head hard on two-by-four rafters and then on the ground. Ever since then, according to the Blaines, "He hasn't been the same." And, in fact, "He's different."

So Johnson was now weird, or maybe he was all along. Either way, he was in our band and starring in our upcoming Super-8 sci-fi horror action movie. While casting we realized we needed someone who could believably be from outer space and would do all kinds of stupid and crazy things. Johnson was perfect for the part: he would do whatever we told him to. The movie was a good thing to do, because, while making it, I could hang out with both my mod and punk friends.

One Step Beyond

Lights, Camera, Vomit!
"At the Movies" by Bad Brains

We went to the Blaines' house to get everything we needed for the movie. One of the most important things we needed was good realistic puke. We had the Blaines' little fifth-grade brother, Ronnie, help us mix together everything gross that we could find in the kitchen. This was an old family recipe that the Blaine brothers had been making for years. They called it Grandma's Butt. Ronnie began stirring in the peanut butter, the pickles, the mayonnaise, bananas, oatmeal, sardines, mustard, honey, cereal, ketchup, crackers, and olive oil. Everything gross they could find.

Ronnie was funny. Ronnie wasn't his real name. The Blaines never called him by his real name and I don't think the twins had called him by his real name for years. They called him Rainus; they called him Caveman, Dog Face. They called him Fungus, Fetus. They called him Gums, Gumboy, because when he smiled, which was most of the time, you would see way more gums than teeth.

Gumboy always approached us, gums bared, happy as hell, sporting his furry crew cut that crept way down his forehead toward his eyebrows, smiling his brains out, sneaking up behind you, tapping you on the shoulder, letting you know a secret about how he had just blown something up.

"Hey, Mike, come check this out." And he would take me to the wreckage of a potted plant or a toy that he blew up.

Egmus's best friend was there, too, helping with the Grandma's Butt. We called him Chinese Coins. Chinese Coins loved explosives. I'm not talking fireworks. I'm talking homemade bombs. Pipe bombs and shit. Within two years he would donate two fingers to the cause. Chinese Coins was not only an accomplished pyromaniac but also a video-game fiend. That was how he got his name. He played video games constantly at the car wash, my old haunt. He would play games there every single day for hours on end. He had amazing skills and became quite respected in the local game community. He played so many games at the car wash that there was no way he could keep up his habit without finding a way in which he could play for free. He was known for using cheap "Chinese" coins that happened to be the same size as quarters. I don't know if they actually were Chinese, but they were foreign. The Blaines just thought it was funny to call him Chinese Coins.

I told Coins about the methods we used back in the day.

I told him about The Battery and the Floss.

"Hey, Chinese Coins," as I mixed some Nilla Wafers into the barf. "You know about the Battery Method?"

"I don't know," Chinese Coins said, all serious and straight-faced, with his bizarrely low voice that had just changed.

"You take a D-sized battery and you slam it as hard as you can right above the change return when the car-wash guys aren't paying any attention. And if you do it just right, in the exact right spot, a game credit will pop on the screen. Bloop."

"Oh, yeah," he said, still straight-faced, serious and not really paying attention. "That doesn't work any more."

"Oh, Coins, that's too bad that doesn't work anymore. We'd never pay. The battery always worked. But we'd get greedy and start pounding the machine, loud as hell, over and over, racking up countless game credits, and the middle-eastern car wash guys would come over and say, 'I'm going to stick battery up your asses, if you don't stop!' Then we'd lay low for a week."

Egmus added some canned oysters and Tim plopped in some mayonnaise and Rick held the mixture to his butt and farted at it.

Then I tried to educate Coins about the "Floss Method."

"Chinese Coins, check it out ... Do you know about the floss?" He nodded yes. "You take some dental floss and you attach it to a quarter with a very tiny piece of Scotch Tape, then you lower it in, dangling it carefully in the coin slot, just far enough (but not too far!), then you doink it up and down and jack up endless game credits."

"Yeah, that doesn't work anymore, either."

"Coins, man, you're screwed. Sometimes we'd get a hundred credits on Pac Man. Then we'd take turns playing for hours, till like 10 p.m." Missing dinner over Pac Man! I'm puking thinking about it," as I stirred the Grandma's Butt.

"I fucking hate video games!" I yelled at Coins. "'I can't beat my high-score! ... I can't beat it! I'm going to kill myself!'"

"No way," he said, seriously. "Video games are the best."

The Grandma's Butt concoction was now finished. We had our costumes and the Super 8 film, so we were ready to shoot.

But we needed a super realistic looking space ship, one that would cost about $100,000. We didn't have a $100,000. Oh good—there just happened to be one down the street from my house sitting in the little park. They were making the TV mini-series "V" in the little park on the cliff that overlooked the ocean.

The TV movie "V" was about initially-friendly aliens, who looked human, but then after you got to know them better, they turned into the nasty reptiles that they really were, and if you were really unlucky you'd have to witness them scarfing down rats and squirrels and other rodents before they murdered you.

The movie crew was up the street filming another scene so we borrowed their space ship, and our movie would be much better than theirs and at a fraction of the cost. Their budget was about five million. Ours was five dollars. We only spent money on film processing (the super-8 film stock was stolen).

The first scene involved Johnson, the alien. We opened close on him. He was bald, naked and shivering. His head was pointed down. He was in deep meditation. He sat with his butt, cold, against a wet lawn. 50 degrees. He hugged his knees in front of him.

The camera pulled back and we saw that he was in the middle of a grassy area. He looked spaced-out, introspective, his mind seemingly a million miles away. The weather was moody and dark with storm clouds. A few big raindrops splattered down.

We filmed a few frames at a time using stop-motion photography, making Johnson appear to whirl around in circles on the grass. Johnson picked up speed; spinning there, eyes closed, head still down. Then we caught a glimpse of a shady character approaching, lurking behind some trees, wearing dark shades, spying on Johnson's activities. Tim Blaine was this man. He darted, carefully, quickly, from tree to tree, sneaking up closer to Johnson.

In an instant Johnson became aware and stopped spinning. He looked up at the man and got up, quickly, distressed. They stared each other in the eye.

Johnson froze for a moment, and then bravely took one step forward, toward the seedy man. The seedy man backed up a step. The alien took another step toward him ... getting braver. The seedy man looked frightened. The seedy man suddenly stopped, gained some courage and held his ground. Then the seedy man took a brave step forward toward Johnson. Johnson, fearfully, took a step back.

Then the seedy man began running straight at Johnson. Johnson began to run the opposite way, trying to escape, but it was no use. Blaine tackled him hard onto the grass. They struggled and wrestled, fighting, on the cold grass. Blaine uselessly pulled on Johnson's quarter-inch hair trying to stick his fingers in his eyes. Blaine was winning and just about to restrain the naked Johnson when Johnson vanished into thin air. Gone. Blaine looked confused, amazed, bad acting.

Then we saw two secret agent men, Randy and his brother, over at the side of the park by the trees, wearing '60s mod suits, walking quickly, efficient in their purpose, toward the suspicious-looking Blaine. Blaine got up and ran for the edge of the cliff as fast as he could and jumped right off the cliff. The camera ran and looked over the cliff and all we saw was the ocean two hundred feet below.

(Tim had jumped the fence and he had too much speed so he tumbled and crashed through bushes and ice plant down the steep incline. This was all to make it look good. He crashed and burned for fifty feet.)

The next shot was down at the beach. Blaine landed hard, tumbling onto the sand.

(He jumped off the lifeguard station, which we kept out of the shot.) Blaine then doubled over, clutched his stomach, nausea gagged up in his throat, then he heaved and puke all over the sand. This was where the Grandma's Butt came in. We poured a pitcher of Grandma's Butt from the hidden side of his head so it looked real.

Splash, gush and onto the sand!

We zoomed in, focusing on the homemade barf that we were so proud of.

Then, amazingly, Johnson arose from it, struggling out from where the vomit was. (Johnson was buried five feet under in the sand and we expected him to make his way out there, pronto, with no help at all. We buried him deep in the sand, butt-naked. It was one of the most ugly, cold, stormy days of the year and Johnson was buried, naked, in the sand.

One Step Beyond

He had to hold his breath for a few moments too. Either that, or he would breathe in the sand and puke. We had covered his face with sand and then poured the puke on top.

Somehow he managed his way out of there, and just as he got out, wiggling like a giant worm, he took off like a flash for the stormy sea, butt-cheeks jiggling. We directed him to enter the water as quickly and spastically as possible.

He stomped out to sea as far as he could until he was completely submerged. He then held his breath for as long as he could, staying submerged, while we got the majestic shot of just the stormy sea and the angry sky in all its grandeur. What a powerful moment. Actually, we could have just cut the minute he ducked his head under, then he could have got out of the water, and we could have taken another shot of the empty sea for as long as we wanted. Whatever. We were going for naturalism.

Back on the beach, Tim staggered around barfing some more. Then, for the climax, Tim ran off, heading for the rivermouth that flowed from Santa Monica canyon. At full speed he ran and jumped off the seven-foot-high sand-ledge, landing hard and off-balance, stumbling into the four-foot-deep creek bed, tripping and crashing and making a big splash as he landed against the mucky pollution-packed bottom. Then he got up and fiercely waded himself into the dark maddening storm-drain. The end. "Brilliant! Incredible!" says Joe Buttlicker of the L.A. Universe.

Eva

"Love Plus One" by Haircut 100

At this point our band was playing a lot of parties. We were having a great time and Violent Attack's following was growing. Many neighborhood kids were getting into it. My life was now the best it had ever been. I was having so much fun being in the band. I loved, and needed, the anger release from playing intense music. At this point I had forgotten about my pathetic loser loneliness due to all the fun and excitement. I was living in the moment, enjoying it, and connecting with a lot of people. I even felt slightly famous. I just didn't feel alone and depressed anymore.

My social life was now the best it had ever been. I had recently met a girl named Eva. Randy introduced me to her one day after school when we were hanging out at the deli. I hung out with her in the afternoons and we slowly got to know each other. From being friends with her I started to feel a little more comfortable and trusting of girls. She was an earthy 11th grader, a natural beauty, and a transplant from Georgia. She struck me as a good person too, very nice. She wasn't so damn sarcastic all the time like so many Palisades girls and Palisades people in general. She had natural dark blonde hair, casual understated clothes. She wasn't trendy and she wasn't a nerd either. She was just a cool girl. She didn't grow up in the Palisades; I thought that that might have had something to do with how warm and non-neurotic she was.

She had a boyfriend, though. But I didn't spend any time being jealous of him or thinking up reasons why she should go out with me instead of him. He was a nice guy and I was happy for him. I was content to hang out with Eva as friends. This was what I needed at the time.

As much as I thought I wanted a girlfriend, I was still too distrusting of women (and all people really). I felt comfortable around Eva and this was helping me. She was warm and caring and a good friend. While hanging out with her I started to realize that I might be able to expect more from relationships; that romance and friendship might be able to be combined.

One day she and I and her best friend went off-roading in Tuna Canyon (the same spot where Randy and I got stuck in the pond at night). It had rained earlier that day, as it had on so many days throughout that fall, and it was muddy and gooey everywhere and there were puddles and ponds all over the place. I made sure this time to avoid the treacherous little lakes. But I had other dumb ideas. I decided to drive down a small, eroded, tilted trail that became increasingly gutted by water run off and treacherous. It got narrower and it started looking like less of a road as we went down it. After a half mile it didn't even seem to be going anywhere in particular anymore. It was totally washed out. I found a place wide enough where I could turn the truck around, and I tried to exit the way we came, but it was too steep and at a thirty-degree angle to the side and we kept sliding into the ditch on the right side. It was so muddy and slippery that when I tried making it up the steep section we kept sliding off into the

One Step Beyond

bush and rock-filled gully on the side. Then it started drizzling. It was a very beautiful late afternoon. One of those rainy days with a mix of darkness and light, streams of sunlight, and dramatic-looking clouds with a lot of shadows around. There were also blasts of wind darting around the hills. What was amazing was that there were so many types of weather happening. It was windy, then calm for a moment, a little light, then dark, cool then faintly warm when the sun shone through. The situation was getting what somebody else might call "worse." The wind was picking up, it was beginning to rain harder, and it was going to be dark in twenty minutes. We were still all smiles, though. I guess we figured we'd probably get out of the mess. But each time we tried to climb the hill, we just slipped and slid right back into the gully.

We started coming close to making it on some tries, but couldn't get over the crest. We didn't have enough traction; it was just too muddy. Every time we thought we might make it out, we slid back into the rut. We tried different tactics. We tried putting bushes underneath the tires. We put the girls in the back of the truck to weigh the rear wheels down, but it was no use. Now we were giddy. We were giggling and laughing, because we were anxious and it was too funny; the sudden gusts of wind and torrents of rain blasted us, and we just couldn't get out! It was now pouring and we were completely soaked. We couldn't get out, but we were coming so close each time, within a foot or two of cresting the hill and gaining the necessary traction to make it over the hump. We all got out of the truck and the three of us just stood there, laughing in the rain. I stood there with a girl on each arm. I turned and kissed Eva on the lips, a nice wet smooch, then (I couldn't believe it!) I turned and kissed her friend for a moment and turned back and kissed Eva some more. This went on for a minute or two, kissing them back and forth. I just thought this was the best thing ever and I was loving life. I didn't care about my truck. I didn't care that I was stuck. I was just joyful. The sky then suddenly got a little clearer and the rain lightened up. The clouds looked Godly and the girls looked like little wet angels, and I felt ecstatic! My life was good! I was wet, muddy and alive. A small waterfall was cascading down the gully on the side of the trail and we splashed each other with the water and laughed for a few minutes about that. Then I got into the truck to try to move it again. This time the wheels grabbed as if there never had been a problem in the first place and we pulled away. Things felt like they were really changing now, this time, this year, this day! Even an irritable punk rocker can look at the sky or the face of a sweet girl and see or sense God. I tasted the sensation of feeling positive about my life and myself. I was feeling hopeful at this point about having a good life; one filled with friends, and love. I'd just keep doing what I was doing, being social, staying busy and something awesome might happen. It was possible I could find a girlfriend.

One Step Beyond

Mike Pearson

One Step Beyond

House Of Fun
"House of Fun" by Madness

It was a Thursday night and the Blaines and I and my friend Big James were drinking beers at a party spot on the bluff called the Manhole. The Manhole was a place where the Blaines often went to drink beer. The party spot consisted of an oversized six-foot manhole with a five-foot wide circle of concrete around that. The circle was perched halfway down some bluffs that overlooked Temescal Canyon near Pacific Coast Highway. It was hidden amongst some trees and foliage. The Manhole was a safer spot for drinking than right on the top of the bluffs. The top had a great view of the bay, but the neighbors would sometimes call the cops when we got drunk and started yelling.

Big James had been a friend of mine off and on since junior high. I had recently introduced him to the Blaines. Big James was six-foot tall, thin, with English-style teeth. James had a way of exclaiming everything in an important way with his hands.

Tim killed his Schlitz Bull Tall, burped loudly, crumpling his can, and chucking it off the cliff. He then tore off another one from the plastic ring. We started talking about the Spook House, which the local park would put on in about a month. The Spook House, also known as The Haunted

House, was held on the two weekends around Halloween at the Palisades' recreational center gym.

Tim said, "Fuck, Big James, so you think they'll let us do a room?"

"Well, man," James said, taking a swig of his beer. "It's all up to Mike Moore. I'll ask him. I'll tell him we want to do a room. I'm The Man there. I've worked there every year since I was ten. I started out as a maze monster. I worked my way up to assistant henchman. I fucking own the place. It should be no problem."

"Halloween's coming fucking soon," I interjected. "We just have to come up with a killer idea for a room."

"Call up Mike Moore tomorrow!" Tim said, burping out the words loudly.

"Okay," James said.

"And leave all the evil ideas to me," Tim added.

Palisadian kids always looked forward to the Spook House. An assortment of guys from the town, twenties to middle age, would get together and build it. Everyone loved the Spook House. It was a Palisades tradition. It was a dark maze that looped around throughout the gym; it was definitely scary, dark and confusing. When you stepped in there it was like another world. It was so dark and disorienting that it felt like you were going through strange passageways. Once you were inside it was hard to imagine it as a gym. As you voyaged through it you would come upon gory horror scenes happening in the different rooms. There were many monsters that you would encounter throughout, and there were strobe lights that pulsed hypnotically and cobwebs strung around that would get in your face. The music was throbbing, nerve-wracking and insistent.

As an elementary school kid, I remember the Spook House being plain terrifying. I would go every night that it was up. I'd ride my skateboard there in ten minutes—it was two miles away, up hill, and I'd be dripping with sweat by the time I got there, all excited.

During junior high, I would hang out there the whole time they were building it, handing guys nails and stuff. When it was up—oh my God!—it was the perfect opportunity to smoke pot and hold hands and hug frightened teenage girls. My friends and I would scare the girls by touching them and then comfort them as they passed through the maze while screaming at the top of their lungs the whole time.

At thirteen I was still scared out of my wits by the infamous Blood Monster who would jump out at us screaming and tormenting us with his chain saw, threatening to chop us up, during the finale, as he chased us out the exit.

I knew that the Blood Monster was just a big guy wrapped in bandages and covered in fake blood, revving up his chain-less chain saw, and that he never really killed anybody, but he still scared the hell out of me. It was easy to believe that he might kill you because the guy put everything he had into his performance. He acted so intense and violent.

At fourteen I became a Maze Monster. Maze Monsters are usually 10 to 14 years old. They get dressed up, with makeup, creepy, as skeletons, zombies, hunchbacks, witches, werewolves, trolls and so forth. The teenage Maze Monsters would often smoke out with friends and lurk around in the darkest spots of the maze, and when patrons came through they would terrorize them and play tricks on them. They would race around unsupervised and undetected, making their presence known just enough sometimes to creep people out. That goose bump feeling of, "I think there's something there, but I'm not sure."

They would sprinkle water and put cobwebs on people and touch them lightly like bugs. Then they would disappear, darting off to another part of the maze. You could barely detect them in the darkness of the maze. You just felt that they were there. You would only see a Maze Monster when they were near a dim filtered light or a strobe.

Sometimes instead of just yelling, "boo!" maze monsters would get crazy and push and rough up smaller kids. Sometimes a maze monster would mistakenly push a big kid; then the big kid would catch the little ghoul and beat him accordingly.

The Spook House was a complicated and difficult thing to pull off. The structure was like a house, a frame built out of two-by-fours covered with plywood. And it had so many weird lights and effects involved. Young carpenters from around town (such as the Canyon Kid Men) got together to build it. They put a lot of pride, time and effort into it.

They did it for the sense of accomplishment, and also because it's fun to see the look of terror, dread and misery on those little kids' faces as they walked through one super disturbing experience after the other. As people get older (and they're not so easily scared anymore) then it becomes their duty to terrorize the young and not-yet-jaded. It's a pleasure and thrill to see the look of horror on their faces.

As a youngster, I demanded to be emotionally traumatized. I took the Spook House very seriously. It was like a holy place to me. Some kids would try kicking the monsters in the balls all defiantly. Not me. I would just stand there obediently with a monster in front of me, scared shitless, kissing monster ass, "Yes, Mr. Monster, sir, I shall gladly lick the caked blood from your balls."

But now we were older and could create our own rooms. We were the next generation of tormentors. Now we would have the control. It was time to give something back to the community. Our mission was to concoct a room that no child would soon forget.

We went to one of the Spook House pre-planning meetings that was held on a weeknight in the room at the back of the gym.

Big James and Tim and I got there early. We sat patiently at the folding tables enjoying the fluorescent lighting and metal mesh over the windows handball-accident-prevention atmosphere. Carl, the nerdy brains behind the Spook House's technical infrastructure walked into the room like the legend he was to us. We gave him our complete attention and respect. He immediately launched into his hyper-technical account of how it was coming along. Genius Carl was so damn scientific about all of this that it was hard to understand just what the hell he was saying. He took off his thick old glasses, rubbed his eyes and got more in depth.

"The Ghostizer is giving us some problems. I'm pretty sure it's just the cathode reactor. If not, the Jizstimator system could be down interminably. Also, the Screaming Skull is glitching on enunciation and its eyes aren't hypnotizing properly. Bill, we need a four-hundred-foot extension cord with surge protector so we can come from Outlet 17 ... That could be some octopus, let's just hope the guys at Station 69 don't come over and jot it. They'd shut us down in a nanosecond. I say build a box over it."

Basically, I think he was just saying the usual: that the wiring and lighting and special-gizmo effects were barely going to be ready on time—if at all—which is what he said every year. It's funny, because it was always the same; there's so much to do and they always work around the clock the last day or so and end up finishing just in time for opening. Carl would always work on it in the dark even after it was opened to the public. Nobody ever noticed the nerdy thirty-something single guy trying to rig a Death Head in the dark by himself.

And every year the music they played was always the same. It played constantly as the Spook House was going up, while it was in action, and while they broke it down.

It was mostly 1970s German horror movie music, like the Dawn of the Dead soundtrack by Zombie. But the one thing they played over and over was Bach's heavy, deathlike pipe organ piece, Toccata in Fugue in D minor. I loved that.

NEENNER-NEORR! Noonn, Ninnn, Noonn, Ninnn, Nunn, Neorr ...

NEENNER-NEORR! ...

So we were about to pitch the idea for our room to Carl and park director Mike Moore when something truly disturbing happened.

A kid I knew from elementary school, he was the full pocket-protector nerd then, but in junior high he got into rock and roll, and he learned how to play the drums, and he got into some bands, and now he was considered kind of cool, but he got too into coke, and he pinned out too much ... Life in the fast lane. Boo Nin Niner Now Nin-Noo Noon Noo Noo ... Boon Niner-Niner Now Noo ... But I digress...

Anyway, it was weird, because I knew him from elementary, when he had an abacus and was into model plane building. He was the kind of kid who drew technical pictures of ships and nuclear subs and fallout shelters. I knew him from the Cub Scouts. His Grandma, who he lived with, was our Den Mother. I don't know where his mom was—she had disappeared a long time ago, maybe off on drugs. Now he was into drugs—acid, coke, you name it. Mostly coke. Now he could drill holes in his wooden Cub Scout Pinewood Derby racer and smoke rock out of it. This was really sad to me. He was a nice kid and he had gone off the deep end.

Everyone in the meeting was trying to ignore what was going on outside by the ping-pong table. It was an escalating argument between my old Cub Scout buddies, Bruce and Jim. It was a shouting match that went like this:

"Goddammit, Bruce. Give me the money!"

"I told you. I don't have it, Jim!"

"Now. Give me the money, Bruce. I don't want to have to hurt you."

"I told you, I don't have it!"

"Give it to me, Bruce!"

"I told you, I don't have it! I told you, I don't have it!"

It went on like that for sometime, over and over.

"He doesn't have the money, Goddammit!" Blaine yelled out the window.

We tried to get back to the discussion, but the argument heightened, and the guy started chasing Bruce around the handball courts and ping-pong table.

Then Bruce came flying into our meeting room. Bruce raced to my side of the room, tennis shoes screeching to a halt. We were all sitting in a circle at four pushed-together folding tables, and he stood there next to me, breathing heavily, sweating profusely, and looking like his world was falling apart. He faced the door that he just entered. Jim was standing opposite in the doorway, just like something out of an old western. They both stood there thinking about their next move, huffing and puffing.

Jim looked enraged! Bruce leaned over, his hands resting on his knees, while he tried to get his breath. A big drop of sweat landed on the table next to me.

It looked like it was going to be one of those chase the guy around the table routines. Hopefully it wouldn't get to the point of Bruce actually taking off across the tables.

We just waited, quietly and patient, for a resolution. Then they started with it again.

"Goddammit, Bruce. Give me the money!"

Not this again.

"I told you! I don't have it!"

Jim chased Bruce around the tables half a lap and they traded sides.

"Bruce! Give it to me!"

"I told you I had to sell the stereo, Jim!"

Bruce! I'm going to kick your ass!"

They started running around the tables like maniacs and Big James was yelling, "Get out! Get out! Get out!" adding to the insanity. Bruce made a last ditch effort for the door when Jim was on the opposite side of the tables, but Jim rocketed after him out the door. After a second or two we heard the sound of poor Bruce getting tackled onto the cement. Then Jim began slugging him over and over. Jim had been his best friend for years. What had Bruce done to deserve this? Was Jim's behavior helping matters? Bruce screamed out crying for Jim to stop.

"Aaggh, Jim!"

"That was my fucking stereo you sold!" Jim yelled.

"Stop, Jim! Stop ... "

Damn! I used to trade Wacky Packs with Bruce. That was depressing. I wished that Bruce would get some help.

But we had a Spook House to build. That would at least keep me out of trouble for a while. We then pitched our room idea, James doing most of the talking. After we were done, Carl and Mike Moore just sat there, looking stupefied, scratching their chins. These were the guys who would yea or nay it.

Mike Moore said thoughtfully, "It's certainly demented, and a bit too sick, perhaps. Pushing the limits of bad taste, and there will definitely be complaints, but I like it."

Carl seconded the motion. We were on.

Tim had come up with the sick idea, and Big James and I helped flesh it out. Tim told us about his idea when we were at Pali High at lunch. Big James was in his first year of Santa

Monica College with me but he also still hung out at Pali during lunchtime.

Tim said, "Do you know what a fuckin' iron maiden is?"

"Uh, a stupid heavy metal band?" I said.

"Hey, don't let Rick hear you say that. He secretly worships them."

"They suck!" blurted out Big James with the last word on the subject."

Tim said, "An iron maiden is like a big..."

"Yeah, we know what an iron maiden is," I said.

So the centerpiece of our room was to be an iron maiden. Band practice was now on the back burner. We had a Spook House to build. We worked every single night for two weeks from 6 p.m. till one in the morning.

The Spook House opened. The first group had entered the maze. We were pumped with anticipation. The group was in the first room. Ours was the second room. The first room was a mad doctor cutting a man in half. We nervously waited for them to enter into our room. I hoped that our room went well.

Big James was dressed up like Alex from A Clockwork Orange. He was wearing all white with long underwear and a hard jockstrap cup on over his pants. He had on a mask with a six-inch nose and he carried a cane.

I was dressed like a freak, pure and simple. I had my white-bleached, spiked hair, which glowed in the fluorescent black light. I wore a red and black striped psychotic '70s shirt, and black Levi's with big, white, bleached splotches all over them, and many earrings, purple high tops, and death makeup.

Curtis, our tall (6' 4") and skinny friend played Happy Clown. He was dressed in a clown costume with a big fluffy orange clown wig, and his face was made up like a traditional clown with a twist. The catch was that he wasn't happy: he was miserable! He looked like most clowns except his smile was upside down and he had giant traumatized eyes with big teardrops under them. The only instruction we gave him was to frown and cry a lot and act terrorized.

To add to the demented mood, we had two fourth-graders, a boy and a girl, with dead-child nuclear ghoul makeup on, in a shopping cart, chewing on two big rotting cow leg bones that Curtis got from his job at the super market. We had a bunch of meat slivers, too, laying all around, hanging off the sides of the shopping cart. It was sick.

The meat got old and rancid real fast, because it was about 90 degrees in there. After a couple days, the rotten meat stench was so bad that people began to complain that it was making them nauseated. How great. Our argument to Mike Moore was that no Spook House was complete without the stench of dead meat. He told us to get rid of it but we kept it through that night. Then the next day a dozen or so people who worked there confronted us and told us that we had to get rid of it. So we told them that we threw it out and hid it. The next day the cow legs were back in the grocery cart with the kids.

It never made us nauseated, though. We liked it. Actually, we got used to it. We spent so many hours in there that we could hardly smell it anymore. Then Mike Moore started yelling at us. He said that there were complaints from everybody, and he ordered us to get rid of it. The stench had already permeated the whole Spook House, though. It had soaked into the wood. There wasn't any ventilation in there. A few patrons had become sick to their stomachs and had to leave.

The first group of Spook House patrons entered our room from the darkness of the maze. As the patron's eyes adjusted, they saw surreal, demented, fluorescent smiling clown faces on the walls. Curtis, Happy Clown, had painted them on butcher paper and hung them. There was a black light and a strobe that blinked in a psychotically disorienting way. A butcher paper banner read in big carnie letters:

"The House Of Fun."

Curtis had painted some great freakish art.

Big James acted civilized as he motioned them into the room, then he jumped forward and got in their faces, Clockwork Orange style: "Good evening friends. How are you doing this evening?" he said, with a mix of joy, psychosis and condescension. I was standing, frozen against the wall incognito, and then I jumped out: "How are you?" I blurted out, like a total asshole. Big James continued: "I would like you to meet my friend, Happy Clown." Big James grabbed Happy Clown forcibly by his clown-suit and swung him into the scene. Happy Clown frowned and wept at that crowd with a face full of deep anguish.

"Happy Clown isn't very happy today," Big James said. "Are you, Happy Clown?"

Happy Clown was emotionally wrecked. He whined and moaned and blinked, frantically crying. "Are you? Happy Clown?" James demanded.

I stepped forward and yelled, ordering him to stop:

"HAPPY CLOWN!"

He stopped crying and looked bewildered.

James and I then grabbed Happy and we roughed him up badly against the wall. Big James hit him with the cane and I socked him in the stomach. Then Big James stepped forward and smugly addressed the crowd again:

"Happy Clown isn't very happy today, because his friend here is going to have to die." Happy Clown looked to the audience for help. Big sad eyes, a crinkled up mouth, holding back the tears, whimpering ...

"SHUT UP!" I yelled in his face.

The whole time I was grasping on to an exhausted recently tortured, half-alive, Tim Blaine, who was dressed pretty much the way he always dressed, Mad Max world punk. We roughed up Happy Clown some more, and then we took Blaine, beating him up some more, and put him into the iron maiden, which stood up against the wall on the right. The iron maiden was a huge stand-up coffin. We opened the door and kids gasped when they saw about a hundred, thick, foot-long nails, sticking out of the door. They were the biggest nails we could find.

Happy Clown was in the corner cowering as we struggled to put Blaine into the iron maiden. Blaine lashed out violently, swinging his arms and kicking.

"NO! NO! NO!" Blaine shouted.

"YES!" I said.

James and I forced him in there and we began to close the door on him. We had to push real hard, because it wasn't easy to get those big spikes into him. We heard gurgling and screaming sounds coming from inside the iron maiden. Parents were mortified that their small children had just witnessed this heinous act. Then Big James looked over to Happy and said, "Now, let's see your friend, Happy Clown!"

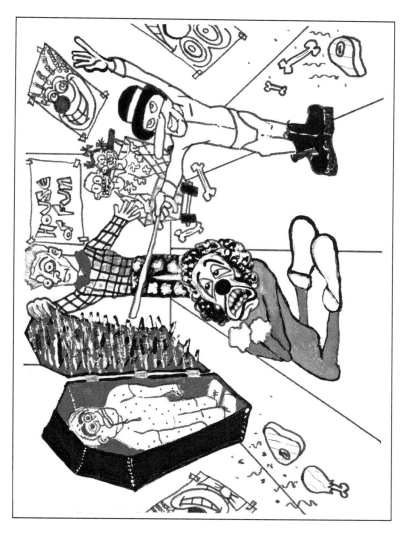

Happy Clown, hesitantly, sadly, opened the door, and out fell Blaine, his shirt riddled with big bloody holes all over.

He fell straight onto the floor without even putting his hands out in front of him; then he began to flop all around violently (and goofy, too), even on to the other side of the audience-boundary rope, right at the feet of all these sickened and disturbed people. He was wiggling there, like crazy, having nasty seizures, and then he did a couple of major body convulsive heaves, throbbed a little bit. And died.

And right when the spectators relaxed, thinking that this horrible display was over, he did one more big fish out of water throb, getting a couple inches of air, his spine straightening out, then he landed and died for the final time.

Then the 15-year-old tour guide with no sense of humor said, "Okay, move this way, please."

They left the room and we laughed our asses off until we realized that the next group was coming.

This is how it worked. The door of the iron maiden opened toward the audience, so it cut off their view of the inside of it. We put Tim into the iron maiden and as we closed the door he went out the back, which was just a black sheet. His twin, Rick (we bleached his hair white so he looked just like Tim) wore the same outfit as Tim but his was dotted with ghastly bloody holes. The dying Rick threw himself out of the iron maiden after we made Happy Clown open it, presenting him.

The twins traded off their dying duties throughout the night. Doing all that falling, flopping and dying was hard work, by the end of each night they were really beat up and exhausted.

Their performances were so hilarious. The convulsions were sick and ridiculous. Sometimes, we'd open the door, and Tim would do a front flip out of the thing and land flat on his back on the floor and then go right into the flopping routine.

When each night was done we'd all go out, drink beer at the top of a mountain and congratulate ourselves to no end, reliving in detail the demented successes of our night.

Mike Pearson

Winter
The Planet Of The Apes
"Ghost Town" by The Specials

It was now winter, December. The winter of '83 was the wettest and coldest one in Los Angeles for a long time. Winters like that only happen every twenty years or so in L.A. It rained nearly every day, and the ground became saturated and the excess water often ran above curb level, making a foot deep river out of streets and sidewalks. A lake had even formed at the top of a dead-ended mountainous street where there was a basin. In the lake there were thousands of tadpoles. Soon the lake overflowed and the tadpoles spilled over the top of the basin and they went flowing down the streets and curbs. They raced along the curbs and were swallowed into the catch basins. They finally glided through the storm drain to their deaths in the ocean.

Big James and I stood in front of his house talking. Without thinking, we began collecting the tadpoles in our Big Gulp cups, then we realized there was no way to save them so we put them back in the gutter to die. The water that had sustained their lives so far had become too much and there was nothing to hold them and keep them safe. There were no shores or safe boundaries or limits. There was nowhere to go but out. They hadn't yet developed into frogs. They were too young and premature. They had to perish. It was their fate.

I didn't want to go out like a punk tadpole. I wanted to have a good life, not a short, stunted, shitty one. I was hoping I didn't get myself killed for some reason with these fucking Blaines. They were crazy and I was a bit concerned.

At this point the Blaines and Big James and I started going on Friday night expedition hikes to a place we called The Planet of the Apes. It was a few miles up a canyon that branched off from Santa Monica Canyon. You could get to it by driving through a very rich neighborhood north of Sunset Boulevard in the Riviera. We took the winding streets as far as we could up into the hills, and went down a fire road. The real name of The Planet was Camp Josepho. Decades before it was known as Murphy's Ranch.

Randy Young, a Palisadian historian wrote that the place was originally constructed in 1939, and that it was designed to be a self-sufficient 50-acre ranch community for Nazis, the brainchild of an insane Nazi named Herr Schmidt who believed that Adolph Hitler would eventually succeed and take over the world. Winona Stephens, heir to a mining fortune, and her husband, a wealthy engineer, fell under the spell of Herr Schmidt, and they spent $4 million to build the ranch.

The Stephens and Herr Schmidt believed that once Germany emerged victorious in the war, Camp Josepho would be a command center for the Nazis who then would emerge from their mountain retreat and impose order on America.

At the time I didn't know who the creators of Camp Josepho were, but I knew they were at least a little nuts. I guess that's why we were attracted to the place; it was just a crazy surreal place to explore and party at.

All the structures were overgrown and spooky and hidden now. That was why we called it Planet of the Apes, because it seemed like some kind of crazy lost civilization. There were cement perches on the sides of the canyon for armed watch guards. We were amazed by the place. It was somehow peaceful and beautiful there, yet it had a dark vibe as well. Maybe that was just coming from our own psyches. But the place did have a creepy history. Maybe that history permeated the place. The place was failed negativity, so in a way maybe it was a positive place, a triumph over man's evil tendencies. Nature was in the process of erasing their demented efforts. Everything was dilapidated and gutted by fires and covered with foliage.

There were a dozen or so concrete staircases that crept up the hillsides. The hill above the ranch had been terraced and equipped with an automated sprinkler system that had irrigated many types of fruit and nut trees. All of that now was almost completely hidden and overgrown with vines and bushes.

There was a bunch of creepy shit still around, though: a communications room, for speaking with Germany, a barn and plenty of fenced in space for livestock, many bomb shelters, a now gutted 400,000-gallon concrete water tank, and a generator station that used to be equipped with double generators that had enough output to power a small town, which this was.

Around the time the ranch was completed the neighbors reported to the FBI that Para-military operations were going on there. Herr Schmidt's dream came to an end the day after the bombing of Pearl Harbor, when federal agents stormed the compound and arrested him and the other Nazis.

The Blaines, Big James and I discovered the ranch at night. We didn't know the story yet behind what we had found. We encountered some of the different elements as we hiked through the canyon in the dark without flashlights. Our only supplies were beer. We were pretty freaked out as we stumbled across the dilapidated barn and the generator station. Every structure at the Planet was entangled with branches and vegetation. There were hidden rooms and the bomb shelters were dangerous because you could fall into them by accident if you weren't careful when exploring. On one trip Tim fell right into one.

As we hiked along, the canyon was dark and bewitching. The barn was red and looked haunted and demonic. I walked past it casually, like I had no interest in going in. I was hoping the Blaines wouldn't want to explore it. Nobody argued with me to go in, thank God. We did go in the generator station. The huge metal doors were slightly ajar and beckoning us. That was the scariest part of the whole experience. That was why we started calling the place "Planet of the Apes," because that structure looked like something right out of Beneath the Planet of the Apes.

On our second expedition to The Planet, it was me, Tim, Big James, Randy, Kaboobie's girlfriend, Audrey, and her friend Elaine. Tim led the way in the darkness down the eroded fire road trail into the canyon. The trail wound its way down one side of the canyon. There were some mud puddles spotting the trail. We descended deep into the canyon and began hiking along just a bit up from the side of the bulging creek. Vines and bushes clawed onto the trail in front of us.

We still refused to bring flashlights with us: that would be considered "wimping," as defined by the Blaines.

We arrived at the canyon floor, and it was nearly pitch black because of a canopy of trees blocking out any light from the night sky. We couldn't see twenty feet in front of us. There was a little fogginess and no moon. The girls switched off holding onto either Big James or me as we made our way down the narrow trail. We made it to the first scary destination at the Planet, the burned-out building. We approached the skeleton, which was mostly a red-painted, rusted metal frame with ripped metal pieces covering it. It looked like something out of hell. It sat in the middle of the clearing and the trail went straight toward it. It looked like it was waiting for us. That was enough for the girls. They wanted to go back. We didn't blame them. The thing was so scary to even look at. We didn't even think of going in it. We were okay with leaving. We'd been out there for a couple hours and had enough fun for one night.

I couldn't get over how great of a place it was to bring girls. The fear factor encouraged hugging and closeness and we could act like strong brave protectors.

Later that week we began planning our biggest expedition yet. We told everyone we knew, all the punks, the mods, new wavers, basically everybody we knew at Pali. The plan was for everyone to meet at the top of the street at the fire road on the next Friday night. People would park at the trailhead, and everyone would drink and hang out there at the overlook for an hour or so, then we would all hike down the descending trail to the Planet. I would collect donations and make my usual trip to the liquor store in Santa Monica where the owners sold to me without carding. I would buy as much beer as I could. We estimated that about twenty people would come on the voyage, but word caught on, and everyone got excited and told each other, so now about forty people said they wanted to go.

On the day of I went by the high school to give directions and invite people personally. It was getting more and more complicated. I gave directions but they couldn't really understand where it was. I then mistakenly agreed to meet different groups of people at different times and places and lead them up there. I was stretching myself too thin.

I was supposed to meet all these different people at different times. I was thinking about how I was going to manage it all when this kid we called Captain America (because he was so all American clean-cut handsome looking) told me that there was a girl who liked me. And this girl happened to be beautiful and popular, and a lot of guys were in love with her, and girls were jealous of her but found her hard to hate because she was really friendly. She was a good friend of the girl who used to sit at the bus stop by the gas station. She was in the girl's swim team group. The swim team girls were all pretty and cool and interested in cutting edge new wave music, punk and mod. I had put that group out of my mind since I first saw them. I didn't even think about them. They seemed just too cute and popular and together. Especially the one who liked me, she was the classic All American Palisades beauty that guys fantasized about, and she was smart and rich too.

"Are you sure?" I asked. "Valerie?"

Captain said, "Yeah, dude, she likes you."

"No way. You're kidding, right?"

"Yes, dude, Valerie likes you."

"Huh?" I said.

I was stumped. "Valerie," he said. 'From the swim team." Then he raised his hands, frustrated with me. "No, actually, that's right, she likes me—I'm sorry, I got confused."

Now I was getting flustered because I had so much to do and I didn't have time to be messed with. Captain America was a handsome lady's man. He was so good looking, with a big smile full of white teeth, a head full of straight blond hair. He looked like a waspy mod super hero.

"No seriously," he said. "Go talk to her."

I hadn't found out about a girl liking me who I was really excited about in … I couldn't even remember. Had it ever happened? No. I liked her. I knew I wanted to be with her. Of course it was for superficial reasons: her beauty, charm, popularity and coolness. How shallow of me. Oh well. I needed to be compelled in some way, or I just wasn't going to go for a girl. I had too much ambivalence toward women (or dread) from my hideous enmeshment with my mom and my glomming grandma, so I needed to be compelled. Valerie, I was going to go for. And she seemed nice and warm and friendly.

Then, when I realized it was true that she liked me, I got so excited that I was filled with butterflies and my face was hot and my heart was beating rapidly. I had to take a walk around the campus to process the feelings and try to calm down. I went over the evidence in my mind that hadn't previously registered. She did smile a lot whenever I was over there talking to her group. She did look at me a lot. As a matter of fact she would look at me for a long time. Just then I glanced over at her group and she was smiling at me at that moment!

"Oh my GOD! Okay, get it together, man, don't freak out!" Then I thought, "What does she see in me? Does she think I'm cool? Why does she think that?"

There I was standing there with my long black trench coat, my white spiked hair, looking kind of like Sting in Quadrophenia. "Maybe I am kind of cool?" I thought. Then I panicked: "But shit, I'm not all mysterious like I look! I hoped she was not expecting me to be all super cool. That's not me! Fuck!" I calmed down again, "Well, regardless, "I've got to ... give ... it ... a try!"

I wasn't confident by any stretch of the imagination, but I wasn't as pathetic as I used to be either. Recently I had gained some confidence. I was now able to talk to people more easily. Being accepted by all the new kids sure had helped. A lot of people liked and accepted me and that had given me strength.

I walked right up to Valerie and her friends. I told them about The Planet and what it was like, where it was, and that they should go. Valerie had a big beaming grin on her face. I started getting all excited again with butterflies. I felt like I was about to jump out of my skin. I was blushing for sure. Valerie said she and her friends had a plan to watch The Who's "Farewell Tour" (their first one) at their friend's house, but after it was over they wanted to meet up. I told them that I could meet them at their friend's house at 10 p.m., and they could follow me to Camp Josepho.

My next thought was, "This is going to be hectic!"

I was going to do everything that I had planned and then go and get them. I would get the Blaines and Big James and get beer. And I promised other groups of people that I'd lead them up there. I'd do that. Then I'd go get Valerie and her friends.

I spent from 6 p.m. till 10 p.m. racing all over the Westside in my truck. I finally herded all the people to the fire road entrance. From there, they could stay there at the view, or walk down the trail toward the canyon, whatever.

Oh, shit, I was late! I hauled ass over there. I was twenty minutes late. They were gone. My gut was turning over. I was so upset. Did I just blow this? I began to beat myself up about it. I had spent so much time trying to make everyone else happy that I didn't make sure to take care of myself. Shit! I should have made sure Valerie was my top priority and that I was on time. I was pissed off and then depressed. I didn't even want to go anymore. I just felt like giving up on the whole thing and going home, but many people would be there waiting for me, and expecting me. I had to go back up there and I was in such a bad mood, so I stopped at the Mobil station in the center of town, bought milk, a candy bar and pretzels, and I sat there on the curb next to the gas pump basking in misery.

Then I saw a blue Chevy Blazer pulling into the gas station. Valerie was driving and the girl from the bus bench was shot gun. What? What were they doing here? They were driving and must have seen my truck in the gas station lot. Valerie pulled her Blazer right up to where I was sitting. I got up and went to her.

Valerie was smiling but the bus bench girl looked pissed off.

"I'm sorry you guys," I told them. "I was so busy and I couldn't get up there in time. I went there, and you guys were gone. I was bummed."

"We thought you were an asshole," bus bench girl said. "We thought you bailed us." Then a smile formed on her face. "But you're here. We found you. That's so cool."

I thought: "Good. They think I'm an asshole. Great. Well, this could be a plus." I had a theory that most girls liked assholes. My next thought was, "Uh oh, what happens when they find out that I'm actually really nice—and probably too nice? Don't be too nice, now, you asshole! Stop it!—Be nice." Then I told myself to just stop thinking. It just wasn't working for me.

I then led them up to Josepho. We got up there at 11 p.m. About fifty kids were at the overlook partying in the dark. I was ready to lead them down the path to Planet of the Apes. I tried convincing them to go, but they were having a good time socializing where they were. Only a handful of them wanted to go down to the Planet. Maybe it was too scary. Also, curfew was coming soon for many of them, so they were content to just hang out at the view with their friends.

The ones who really wanted to go to Josepho were the punkers, Tim and Rick and their friends. Rick couldn't wait any longer so he headed off with five of his buddies down the trail after yelling "Pussies!" at all the people he couldn't convince to come.

Generally I liked and appreciated outcasts and rebels, but Rick went too far in pushing people away. He was so antagonistic. Tim made at least some effort to talk to different people. Hardly anybody liked Rick, though, and he always did something harsh to alienate himself. He seemed to enjoy being the quintessential outcast asshole. He was very insulting and in a way he was challenging people to get to know him and find out he wasn't such an asshole after all. He reminded me of Klaus, and my dad. He was harsh but on some level he wanted to be liked. To most people, Rick was just a jerk and they would leave it at that. Rick only hung out with the outcasts, the losers, high IQ glitchers, and anti-social creeps—the disturbed kids. Pretty much all had been neglected and abused to some extent. After Rick and his weirdo group left, I spent some time talking and flirting with Valerie. She leaned up against my truck. She was sexy! We drank some beer and she told me her story about the night Rick and his friends ended up on the lawn with makeup all over them. It was she and her friends in the car that sped away. She told me how Rick and his buddies messed up her friend's house and that that was the least they could do to get back at them. I then asked Valerie if she wanted to go for a ride to the bottom of the canyon in my truck and see the Planet. She was definitely willing. We had about an hour and a half before she had to take her friends home.

The fire road that led down to the bottom of the canyon was such an eroded mess, but I wanted to be awesome and drive down it. I locked my front wheel hubs and shifted into four-wheel-drive. We took off down the trail. The road was treacherous, narrow in spots, and washed out, like the trail I went down with Eva, but not as bad. There was a cliff on one side and a mountain on the other. There were lots of ruts and rocks, with some boulders that had fallen from the hillside, and the thing was, that, when you got near the bottom, the fire road suddenly ended and dropped off a cliff. There was only one place wide enough to turn around. You could drive past that point to the end of the road but then you'd have to back out for a quarter mile until you got back to the place where it widened. The trail wasn't that difficult to drive down in the day, but at night? And the Schlitz Bull talls would make it tougher. I told myself to drive slowly and carefully. (People drove drunk a lot back then; it wasn't until the late '80s before I even heard of the concept "designated driver.")

So it was Valerie and I and her best friend Norma and Tim. Bus Bench Girl got a ride home with other friends. After bucking down the road for ten minutes we came across Rick and his buddies, and we passed them. They each carried their own twelve packs. I drove past the turn-around spot. Then I got worried that I might end up too drunk to back out. I figured we had better go back now to the wide spot now and turn the truck around. Then I could reverse my truck further down the trail, but at least it would be facing the right direction. Then we would hike down to the Planet and when we came back I could just drive out.

As I reversed we came across Rick and his friends again. They were inebriated and acting belligerent, throwing rocks and breaking bottles. None of them were walking straight. They were stumbling all over.

"What are you guys doing?" Rick slurred. I said, "We're trying to back up to that spot up there so I can turn around. I don't want to do it later when I'm more fucked up."

"There's a spot right up there, man. This way. Check it out."

"I know. I see it," I yelled.

He began guiding me to back up toward him.

"Come on, man," he said. "This way."

I wasn't paying any attention to him; I was concentrating on the spot fifty feet or so behind me where I was going to crank the truck around. I was keeping my eye on the cliff and aiming my truck. Rick was behind me on the passenger side, motioning, but I couldn't see him because of my truck shell that created a huge blind spot. I could just hear him yelling.

"All right, good, you got it. More. Okay, this way, all right, good. You got it. Come on back."

The turn-around spot was right behind me now. I quickly cranked the truck around—

Bonk!

"What was that?" I asked. "Uh oh. I must've hit something." "OWWWH!"

"That sounded like Rick. Oh, my God, I must've hit Rick. Oh, no!" My heart started beating. "Maybe he was joking. Oh man, I couldn't have hit him. I was going fast too."

"OWWWH!" we heard again.

I turned off the truck, pulled the emergency brake, and we all got out to see what happened. Where the hell was he? We didn't see him anywhere. He wasn't on the trail. I looked under the truck. Good, he wasn't there.

"Unggh ... " we heard a groan coming from somewhere. Tim ran around to the back of the truck.

"Where are you?" Tim yelled.

"You fucking hit me, Goddamn it!"

Another pause. I was really worried now. Then I asked hesitantly, "What?"

"I'm fucking down here!" he yelled.

We looked to where the voice was coming from; it came from down in a deep, dark bush-filled gully at the mountainside of the trail.

"Are you okay?" I shouted into the pit.

"My leg! You broke my fucking leg!" we heard the gully reply.

I thought, "Oh, no. Bullshit. I couldn't have? Did I?"

I was really worried, but I also began laughing out of nervousness. It seemed so ridiculous: one minute he was guiding me, the next minute he was in a pit.

Then I got defensive. I told the girls: "I didn't ask him to guide me. I needed to look the other way, to avoid the cliff."

Tim and I lowered ourselves into the rocky gorge. Rick was lying there at the bottom of the gully, lying amongst some bushes and rocks. We picked him up and carried him out. We put him down and he started limping around badly. I felt guilty and sorry for him. I wanted to believe that he was faking it. I wouldn't put it past him to do something like that. You could never quite know for sure with the Blaines; they were always screwing around.

"Just take me fucking home, okay," he said.

We put him in the back of my truck and he just lay there. The girls stayed in the cab waiting while we pretended to be doctors, asking a lot of questions about where and how it hurts.

One Step Beyond

"Oh, no! And things were just about to happen with Valerie!" I thought selfishly.

I figured he might actually be hurt. It was quite a drop into that gully. But what was I going to do? I couldn't take him home! I didn't want this to spoil my night, my whole love life I'd been waiting so long for. I had been waiting forever for a chance with a girl like Valerie. Can't he get one of his friends to take him home? Don't any of those idiots drive? No, they got a ride there from someone else who had already left.

So I let him suffer in the back of my truck while I got to know Valerie better. It was cold of me, but to rationalize, he either suffered in my truck or he suffered at his house. I gave him two beers, one to drink and one to ice his ankle with. I had to spend some time with Valerie before she had to go home. (The next day we found out that he had a sprain; he limped around for a few days.)

It was getting late, though, and guilt was starting to creep in on me. Valerie was going to have to take her friends home anyway now. It was 12:30 am.

I asked Valerie if she wanted to meet up after we dropped everyone off.

"I'll meet you at the Village Green, then I'll drive us back up here.

"Okay," she smiled. Wow. She seemed very willing.

Everyone was leaving now, except Captain America and Elaine. They said that they would stay and wait for us to get back, and then the four of us would hike up to the Planet together.

I dropped off the drunk and wounded. By 1 a.m. I was at that Village Green waiting. The Village Green is a traffic island with a bench, a patch of grass and a couple trees, in the middle of the Palisades Village. It's where the hippies, heshers and "greeners" hung out.

I was there for almost an hour. It seemed like forever. I was just about to give up and call it a night, figuring she wasn't going to show. I was sure Elaine and Captain had already gone home. Then I saw her drive up the deserted street.

I was so happy and excited. I got in her car and we drove up there and surprisingly Elaine and Captain were still there. All four of us set out down the trail.

I had that tingly excited feeling going; the kind you get when you're first with someone you really like, and you feel that something's brewing and there's a lot of anticipation, and you feel like the other person likes you too, but you don't know when (or if) or what exactly is going to happen. But something will…you hope it will!

I was kind of amazed by how brave and trusting the girls were about hiking into that canyon in the middle of the night. They were just walking along, huddled up against us, our arms around them. They were having fun being scared instead of not having fun being too scared. Maybe we were all not so afraid because our excitement about hooking up was overriding fear. And maybe there really was nothing to be scared of. Maybe?

We arrived at the Planet of the Apes generator-station after fifteen minutes of walking and hugging. The atmosphere was spooky the whole way but it was also very romantic.

We slowly entered the cold dark generator station. One by one, we climbed the rusty steel ladder toward the rooftop. We sat on a metal ledge that was perched about five feet beneath the ceiling. It was about fifteen feet off the ground; it had a rail in front of us to hold on to. There was a six-foot by twelve-foot rectangular hole in the cement ceiling near us, and the moonlight beamed in at us, casting strange shadows on the dusty dirty concrete floor.

I put my arm around Valerie and she put her arm around me. We talked about nothing in particular, but it was the best conversation I had ever had, just flirting. I was surprised at how easy it was for me to start kissing her. It struck me that when a girl's interested it's really not a problem. This was the opposite of my frustrating experience pining for little Amy throughout the summer to no avail.

We kissed for about forty-five minutes straight. I really liked the way she kissed! It was soft and restrained when that felt right, and passionate and intense when that felt right. She kissed just the way I liked. I was way into it. I felt like we were on the same wavelength.

Elaine and Captain were kissing the whole time, too. The night had finally turned into something great. At last all the chaos had winded down and it was peaceful, quiet and perfect. It was a great night. Probably the most memorable night of my life up to this point.

She was the most beautiful thing in the world. Short blonde hair, soft young skin, nice beaming loving lusting eyes. I felt so much gratitude. I had always fought so hard for girls. Like it was the hardest thing in the world to get someone to like and want you. This time it just fell into place, easily. Finally—it worked! I knew that we were going to go out, and probably for a while, I hoped.

She was the Dream Girl. I put all of my fantasies of what I wanted from a girlfriend and put them on her. What a load I expected her to carry: being perfect and all, my fantasy come true. The love I could never squeeze out of my parents I would receive from her, because she was loving, caring, sweet, funny and charming and ...

Who was she really, this seventeen-year-old beauty? I didn't know. I didn't know her. All I really knew was that she was super frickin' pretty, I liked the way she kissed, touched, and smiled at me. In her eyes I could see the reflection of what I wanted to see in myself. What was the reality of the situation? I had no idea. It wouldn't be long, though, before our actual personalities and our Issues conflicted with what we had created. The reality wouldn't invade until later, though. For now, she was my creation, my beautiful monster. My idealization fit right over her and I didn't want her to let me down. She was created from my intense longings. She was perfect: Civilized, Savage, Sexy, Spontaneous, Sick, Needy, Sad, Beautiful, Healthy, Loving, Independent, Yearning, Cool, Composed, Caring, Smart but not a Smart Ass, Sexy but certainly not Slutty. Now it was time for her to live up to it, all of it. I wished her luck because she would need it.

It was 3 a.m. when we heard something frightful and horrifying: something that sounded like a wounded animal in the distance, like a screaming wounded thing, like a wild man or a Banshee or something! Don Juan from the Castaneda books might say it was a "spirit catcher."

One Step Beyond

What was it? Could there be a human out here in the middle of the night, in a canyon, a crazy homeless person, perhaps? Then it got louder, sounding like it was creeping closer. We heard its terrible shrieks becoming louder and louder, closer and closer. The shrieks happened about every thirty seconds. What kind of animal could it be? Bizarre thoughts and images raced through my head. I was getting pretty scared now. If it weren't for the excitement of hooking up with Valerie I'd be terrified, not knowing whether to run or freeze in fear. Instead I just sat there, kissing her some more, while listening and aiming one eye in the direction of the open ceiling.

A few minutes earlier it seemed far enough away; the sound was faint enough for us to pass it off as "just a big bird" or something "natural" or "normal."

But now it was closer, and it was shrieking constantly, and every minute or so there would be a loud chilling wailing scream. Was it a ghost or something supernatural? I didn't want an answer to that question. Then it was so close that it sounded like it was just above the generator station on the hillside, a little bit to our left, maybe fifty feet away. We all sat there, frozen, quiet, not knowing what to do. Was it too late to run? We just looked at each other with big eyes as we listened.

It couldn't have been any of the kids from earlier playing a joke they had all gone. Who would be out there at this hour? Not even Rick would think of doing something like that. I wished it was Rick, but he was unfortunately at home with his twisted ankle.

I tried to think of what kind of animal it could be and I came up with nothing. This was Los Angeles, not the

Amazon. There is no bird in L.A. that sounds like that. I figured that we better just leave. I motioned to the others to leave. We descended the ladder, headed out the front door of the generator station, and ran away quickly and quietly. Luckily, whatever it was, it did not follow. The only rational explanation at the time was that it was a homeless person scaring the shit out of us. Years later I thought that it might be a wild boar. But I still like to believe that it was a banshee or spirit catcher.

Whatever this thing was, it marked the beginning of my relationship with Valerie. We were joined in matrimony in a Nazi generator station by the power invested in an angry wailing mutant freak. The freak wanted Valerie and I to be together and it even handled our mating calls for us.

Mike Pearson

One Step Beyond

My Girlfriend Valerie
"Love My Way" by the Psychedelic Furs

The next day after school, and almost every day after for a few months, I went over to Valerie's house. She lived three miles north of me on the top of a hilly neighborhood. You could see the ocean through the eucalyptus trees from her second story bedroom window. Her house was big and nice—about 4000 square feet, three bedrooms, two and a half baths, family room, redwood deck with Jacuzzi, wine cellar, and a canyon view out the back. Both of her parents grew up in Los Angeles. Her dad was a cool, friendly guy, young, in his mid-forties; I thought he was young because my dad was an old 68. Her dad was muscular and thick, like a mountain man, with his big beard. He was a real estate investor and owned a lot of rental properties. Valerie's mom was another story. She seemed angry and bitter and was often critical of her family. Valerie shared a bedroom with her cute, blonde, fifteen-year-old sister. Valerie also had a good-natured thirteen-year-old brother who was into punk and surfing. I got along with her brother and sister right off the bat.

Valerie and I spent most of our time together in the basement family room kissing and watching hours and hours of MTV videos. MTV was new at the time; it had just come out a couple months earlier on the west coast and we thought it was the best thing ever; finally, visuals to go with my music. Back then they played videos day and night. There weren't any shows, just videos. Now we knew what the artists looked like and how they dressed. Every sound and image from the videos mixed and melted into my experience with Valerie. And every song happened to be about Valerie. MTV became the soundtrack to my experience with my girlfriend. This period of time felt fantastical, dreamy and romantic. It felt that way at the time, and it still has that feeling attached to it as I look back. It had a different feeling from my life before that. Romance and fantasy had washed over me. The fact that it was always raining and chilly added to the effect and helped put me in the different frame of mind. Rain and cold was really different for L.A.

Was what I experienced "reality?" It was a version of it, I guess. But it was mostly unreal. I had heightened senses and emotions. I was floating, not grounded at all. The new music of the time and MTV was amplifying it all.

We had been going out for two weeks and it was New Year's Eve and Valerie's seventeenth birthday. Valerie was going to have a sleepover birthday party with all her friends at her house. She asked me to sneak over there late that night. She said it was to be all girls, but I could come after her parents went to bed, around 1 or 2 a.m.

At 2 a.m. I knocked on the French doors at the back of the family room where the girls were sleeping. They were all in their sleeping bags lying in different directions on the carpet. I felt like an intruder. I didn't want to get caught and get on the bad side of her parents. I wanted them to like me. I was nervous about the whole thing.

She unzipped her sleeping bag and motioned for me to get in. I figured that a couple of the girls might be awake eavesdropping. That made me more uncomfortable. There were about ten girls down there. I got on the floor and wiggled into the bag. I started to kiss her. I was very uneasy. Girls all around, but everything was quiet, real quiet. After we kissed for about five minutes, I slid my hand under her t-shirt to her breasts. Her breasts were round and firm, fairly big for her small body, and perfect. I was getting excited. I had felt her breasts once before in my truck while parked on the street in front of her house before she went home one night. She was moaning a bit now, and she opened my pants and started to pull them back and down. I wasn't sure what to do. I was still nervous but I took them off. Her legs were bare. She was in her underwear. Her skin was smooth, soft and perfect. I felt her on the outside of her underwear and she was hot. She reached her hand down my boxer shorts. Damn!

I hadn't done much thinking about this. It now seemed obvious she wanted to have sex. I didn't think it would happen this fast. I figured there'd be some time to build up to it—in a more private setting! I had somehow expected it to take a lot longer to get to this point. I thought I might have to wait a month or two (or maybe six). I didn't know how long. But right now? What was going on? I felt so naïve. I thought she might've been a virgin! I thought maybe she had made out some, but never done it before, or if she had, maybe only once or twice like me and she would be a bit tentative about it. I didn't think she'd be ready after two weeks! I was scared now and starting to sweat a bit. I think I might've even shuddered a couple times. I should've said no with some kind of finesse, because I wasn't ready. We had no protection. I was just going to slip it in there for a while or what?

So I had some awkward nervous sex with her and pulled out in the nick of time. This pretty much set the tone for the rest of our sexual encounters. I was never quite comfortable. I should have just held off that night. But I thought I had to do what was expected of me—and all guys. In addition: it's hard to screw someone properly when they're up on a pedestal.

I projected that she was some kind of innocent eleventh-grade virgin. I didn't know my little blonde baby had a 19-year-old boyfriend the summer before and had had sex plenty of times. Plenty of times, compared to my once!

The tone was set. I was intimidated. And we always had a hard time trying to find a private place to have sex. I didn't like my house because my mom and grandmother were always too nosey. The truck in a parking lot isn't so bad, depending on the parking lot. Sometimes at her house it was okay, but we had to be super quiet because her sister was right next-door and her parents could come knocking at anytime.

One time was horrific. It was a Friday night and we were in her room. Her sister was in the next room, her little brother was downstairs goofing around with some friends, and her parents were down there too. We were kissing in her room, talking and playing records. We put on The Specials, and then we played Selector. Then, after we got more heavily into making out, she asked me what I wanted to hear. I looked through her records, and she had all the Cure albums. I only knew of The Cure because of their current pop hit, Let's Go to Bed, which was playing a lot on MTV. I loved that video: Robert Smith and Laurence Tolhurst, the keyboardist, throwing a ball back and forth to each other in a room, both dressed in white with neon vibrant colors splashed around, and Robert Smith would catch the ball over his shoulder without looking, while singing:

"I don't want it if you don't. I won't play it if you won't play it first ... Oh, oh, oh, oh oh ... Let's go to bed."

I figured all their stuff was like that. I was dead wrong. Let's Go to Bed was the pop hit Robert Smith wrote purposely to get out of the rut of becoming increasingly depressed and death rock. I didn't know about the Cure and their Goth death-rock period. Robert Smith had become increasingly dark, intense and disturbed over the course of their last three albums: Seventeen Seconds, Faith and Pornography. Those three albums, before In Between Days and Let's Go to Bed, were like a death rock trilogy. Stark, sad and minimal, pale and lonely were those albums. Their first album was kind of minimal punk pop, but then came Seventeen Seconds, then Faith, and then the ultimate brutal, death rock album, Pornography. In an interview, he said that if he kept trying to one up himself in gothic death rock he was going to die from drugs and misery; like the guy from Joy Division who hung himself on video. Robert Smith didn't want to die, so he blew that whole death rock thing apart by going all the way to fun pop. He left all his serious depressed music fans in the dust and saved himself from annihilation.

When she asked me what I wanted to hear, I chose Pornography. It seemed appropriate for the situation. The cover of the album should've been a give away for what was in store for me: three ghostly blurred-out skull heads, with black hole eyes, tinted hellishly in red and black.

Not one pop song like "Let's Go to Bed". We had foreplay through "One Hundred Years," the first song on the album, a song about dying a horrible death after a nuclear holocaust. The first words to the song, and the album:

"It doesn't matter if we all die!"

As the music played, and we made out, I began to get more nervous and I started sweating. The anxiety in my chest built through the following songs:

A Short Term Effect, Siamese Twins, The Figurehead, Cold, and Pornography. You get the idea. Don't ask me why I kept going while feeling so uncomfortable. I guess I was used to feeling uncomfortable. I should have taken that disk off and flung it out the window.

I was nervous that family members would come knocking. The room was cold, the music was warped and demented, and we were lying on the chilly floor and my feet were cold.

I don't think I need to tell you I didn't get it up that night.

I attempted during Siamese Twins, and it was like a soundtrack to my plight. The words:

"I chose an eternity of this. Like falling angels, the world disappeared. Laughing into the fire. Is it always like this? Flesh and blood and the first kiss, the first colors, the first kiss. He writhed under a red light, voodoo smile, and Siamese twins. A girl at the window looks at me for an hour, then everything falls apart, broken inside me, it falls apart. The walls and the ceiling move in time. Push a blade into my hands, slowly up the stairs and into the room. Is it always like this? Dancing in my pocket. Worms eat my skin. She glows and grows with arms outstretched, her legs around me. In the morning I cried. Leave me to die. You won't remember my voice. I walked away and grew old. You never talk, we never smile. I scream: you're nothing! I don't need you anymore. You're nothing! It fades and spins. Sing out loud we all die, laughing into the fire. Is it always like this? Is it always like this!"

Now that's the blues.

I became more despondent during songs such as Cold and Pornography.

I picked the wrong album.

I was so nervous as it was. I thought Pornography would've been good for sex. But it turned out to be the most DEATHROCK, HORRIFYING, DEPRESSING, CLAUSTROPHOBIC, DOOM IMPENDING album ever made. That's a good twenty-six depressing songs to be depressed to. Order now.

I told her how the situation made me nervous and uncomfortable, and she said it was okay. But it wasn't. I was disappointed and ashamed.

Our sex life was okay at times, but most often it was stilted. I didn't have any experience and never really became comfortable with her. I don't think we were ever intimate and close emotionally. Our relationship was pretty superficial. I was vulnerable and deep into the relationship emotionally, on a neediness level, but I never really felt safe and free. I was never sure how much she liked or cared about me. We were superficially close but in reality not very connected.

I would eat at Valerie's on most nights. I can't remember what happened with my family at this point. I guess I traded my family for hers. I hadn't spent much time with my family anyway. Now it was none. I didn't miss spending time at my house. In contrast to her house it felt very alienating and lonely. Valerie's family felt more like a real family. I wasn't so crazy about her mom, but I loved her dad. He was a warm and nice guy.

Valerie had to go and do homework every night at 7:30. That's when I went home. She had a 3.9 grade average. She was smart and always did her homework. Her parents expected that of her. I was still doing just enough homework to get by with C's. When I saw her going off to study, it really made me consider doing more homework. It depressed me to think that she was two grades younger and would be getting into a four-year college before me.

My thoughts and feelings engulfed me. Within a few weeks I was inundated by scary feelings of dependence. The fact was I was more in need than in love. The relationship opened up my unmet need pit. I tried to keep from feeling too desperate and dependent, so I would pry myself away from her and spend time with the Blaines and play in the band.

After going out for a month, Valerie, Tim, Norma and I went to a big exciting punk show in Hollywood. TSOL (True Sounds of Liberty), Social Distortion and Youth Brigade were playing. The concert was at S.I.R Studios, a musical equipment rental warehouse on Sunset.

I put Tim and Norma in the back of my camper-enclosed truck bed. Valerie was up front with me. I found a parking spot a few blocks from the warehouse. We walked up the street thinking we were tough. We paid the five-dollar cover and entered. The place was packed with about a couple thousand punkers. Hardcore punk was probably at its '80s peak of popularity in L.A.

At the time a lot of the early punks were still into it, and there were now hundreds of younger people entering the scene. Actually, its newfound popularity among suburban kids was signaling its demise. I felt that it was becoming less authentically punk by the minute. It was now turning into something that kids would get into because it was "cool" and popular. Not cool, as far as I was concerned. It was in the process of becoming rigid and codified, as it got faster and more "hardcore." It was losing its beautiful wild mutant quality. Later, it would have nowhere to go, but grow up, get a job, and make lots of money. But that wouldn't be for about ten years when Nirvana, Green Day and the Offspring would sell millions of punkish albums.

Youth Brigade opened, Social Distortion was second and TSOL was the headliner. I liked TSOL the best out of the three. They were more fun, theatrical and weird. They had a deathly, ghastly apocalyptic approach, done with a sense of humor. In the early '80s there was the obsession with nuclear holocaust. The cold war was on and there seemed to be the possibility of lunatic world leaders blowing us all up.

We pushed through the crowd and settled in the middle of the hall. TSOL were playing super loud in the giant auditorium filled with echoes. They had black, greasy, creepy hair that came down long and pointed in front of their white, pasty faces. They had such a great look with black makeup smeared around their eyes. They looked like nuclear war victims, true ghouls! The place was packed and there was so much energy; people were feeding off the wild energy.

There was a giant whirlpool of a slam pit in the front near the stage. We were in a good spot, just outside of the slam perimeter. I looked around, admiring the crowd, feeling solidarity with, and affection for, the punkers of our city.

Tim went off to go do battle in the slam pit. I stayed with the girls. We watched him grimace and pout as he performed his expert arms-flailing, wild-chicken, speed-skating slam dance. He came back drenched in sweat, with only half his t-shirt. He always ended up with bruised ribs or some damage from stage diving and trying to fly over something and slamming into it.

TSOL were a few songs into their set when we heard from the punks nearby that hundreds of cops were outside. Rumor had it that the L.A.P.D. were trying to crack down on punk rock before the 1984 Olympics. For whatever reason an aggressive and abusive police presence was showing up more and more at shows.

The next thing we knew, the L.A.P.D. cut the band's power off. TSOL just stood there on stage holding their instruments looking pissed off. The lights came up in the auditorium. Everyone waited quietly to find out what was happening. Jack Grisham, TSOL's singer, addressed the audience. Everyone became silent and listened.

He said something like: "The L.A.P.D. are outside wanting to kick some ass. But what are we doing? Nothing! Minding our own business! That's right! If they think we're here to start a riot, they're wrong, because that's not in our nature. We're just here to have a good time! But if that's what they want, and that's what they expect, then maybe that's what they should get! Go ahead and have a good time kids. Have a fuckin' riot!"

So a couple hundred of L.A.'s rowdiest youths responded and went out to do battle with the L.A.P.D. It didn't make any sense to me. I wasn't going out there. Even Blaine didn't consider it. You can't win against guys with guns and bats and chips on their shoulders when all you are armed with is tattoos, boots and considerable amount of anger toward your parents. The kids threw some bottles at cops, they yelled some shit at them, and then they either ran away or got beat up. Then I heard the news that the cops were coming in to disperse the crowd with tear gas. A lot of the punks didn't want to leave because they knew what kind of violence might be waiting for them outside.

Jack of TSOL was really cool and charismatic, kind of like a punk Jim Morrison. He told everyone to sit down and be mellow so when the cops came in it would be like:

"How could you tear gas all these nice peaceful punk-rockers?"

Easy was the answer.

TSOL started playing one of their songs acoustically, no amplification (one that was normally super fast, like all of their songs), but they played it real slow, in an earthy hippie style. It was like the sixties in there. I looked around at a bunch of death rockers, bald and mohawked, tattooed punks who were sitting there peacefully, Indian-style on the floor enjoying the music. This was so odd, but touching in a way. The vibe was: "Hey, man, we're just people, trying to have a good time. Don't let those cops get you down." Punk was the angry son of the sixties.

Punks are usually in a state of mad motion, speaker diving, chicken fighting, and acting like lunatics. It was nice to see them chilling out being humans. Then about a dozen cops entered at the right of the stage. The cops looked confused and didn't know what to do when they saw hundreds of punk rockers sitting there peacefully enjoying the folk music.

So they responded by chucking tear-gas bombs at us.

We quickly exited out the back, avoiding the gas. We hurried along Sunset with hundreds of others. There were thirty or forty squad cars and a hundred or so officers lining the sidewalks in riot gear. They all had shields and were holding batons. They looked like storm troopers. It made me nervous to think that I could get bonked at any moment for no reason and there would be nothing I could do about it. I saw them hitting some rowdy punkers and throwing them into paddy wagons. We saw a kid we knew from the Palisades get thrown in the wagon for kicking a beer bottle. We quickly got to my truck and took off back home.

I felt sorry for Tim. I was still lonely and pathetic with a girlfriend. I figured he must be really lonely. I wanted him to hook up with Norma. One night I was in the TV room with Valerie, kissing her and playing with her breasts when I stopped to have a conversation. I told her that Tim liked Norma, and that they should get together.

"Tim would love to go out with her," I said. "Tim always says, 'Norma's so fuckin' cool.'"

A stunned expression came across Valerie's face and she started laughing.

"Oh, he would, would he? Mike, Norma's not going to go out with him. I'm sorry to say, but Tim is so ugly. And what a personality!"

We both sat there pondering her statement. I thought it was a little harsh.

Then she added: "Plus, he's out of his mind." She started laughing again.

I couldn't argue with that.

I thought it was too bad Norma didn't want to go out with him. I thought it would have been fun to go out and do stuff together as couples. I also felt that it would be nice for Tim to have a girlfriend. It would probably mellow him out some and reduce his rage level some. I already felt more soothed and less pissed off from being with Valerie.

"Is he really that ugly?" I asked.

"Yes. And Tim's not Norma's type," Valerie said, amused.

"What is Norma's type?" I asked.

"Well, she kind of goes for older bald guys."

"What?"

"Don't tell anybody; she's had a crush on Craig Fremont—you know, the surfboard shaper, Dogtown guy, Fremont Designs?"

"That guy! He's forty!"

"He's not that old, he's twenty-seven."

"He is bald."

"He's a nice guy."

"Why's an old guy like that going for Norma?"

"Well, they're an on-an-off again thing. And he's nice!"

"What? What do you mean an on-and-off-again thing?"

"Well, you know; it's kind of complicated."

"You mean he gets on her, then he gets off her again, then on her. That's fucked, man, he's just using her!"

"No, it's not like that. She uses him just the same. We'll go over to his house sometime. You can meet him. He's cool. You'll like him. He always has great parties too."

I looked at her, long pause. "What about Tim?"

"Mike, no one's going to go out with Tim. Drop it." She laughed and hit me with a charming smile.

I felt bad for Tim. It was pathetic. He would end up going out with me and Valerie and Norma when we went out, but there wasn't going to be any romance for him.

It was obvious Tim was infatuated with her, because he was always on his best behavior when around her. What that means is he wouldn't burp in her face or slam doors on her. Tim was the kind of guy who's idea of a nice date was to bring a girl up to the bluffs, tell macho punk rock war stories to her, and make her pound cheap malt liquor. To be honest, that wasn't much different from my idea of a good date.

Tim decided to hang out, patiently waiting for Norma to give him the go-ahead, but the go-ahead never came.

I thought some more about it, "Who would want to go out with Tim? Hmm. Well, he has a few strikes against him. He doesn't have a car. And that's a negative. He's not good looking, and that's a negative. He's very angry and negative. That's a negative." I couldn't come up with anything. Oh well, focus on yourself, I told myself.

My mood was now pretty heavy. Being with Valerie stirred up some deep sadness in me. It had activated old feelings of deprivation and unmet needs. I was ashamed that I felt so needy and desperate and empty. I tried to hide it. I loathed my neediness. She seemed normal and free from that. She didn't seem to crave closeness like I did. On the other hand I would get so scared when I got close that I would pull back and be distant from her.

I was worried that I was becoming too vulnerable. I tried really hard not to be too needy because I figured it would probably get me dumped. This wasn't an authentic relationship. I was not able to be my loser self. I had to try to be cool. In my fantasy world it seemed great at the time—and on paper it looked awesome: hot, popular, punk, blonde chick on my arm. I was king of the Palisades! Whoopee.

I had been with Valerie for a couple months. I was still at her house most days after school watching MTV on the couch. It got dark early and it was still cold and rainy on most days. We always had a blanket over us and a fire was always going in the fireplace. It felt cozy at times but also kind of remote and disconnected. But I wasn't that conscious of that. It seemed good compared to the deprivation I knew before this with my family. I didn't know what I was really missing as far as real intimacy goes.

The videos from the early '80s had the certain strange cold feeling of the time. Most of early '80s new wave was English and had that chilly vibe. The music was cool, detached, like a Kubrick movie. The chilly synthesizer sound added to this.

Fashion, surface and image were now as important as the music itself. In the past you could be an ugly overweight haggard but a soulful and talented musician and have big records. Not so much anymore. Goodbye Christopher Cross, etc. Now, for the most part, musicians had to be good looking, skinny and young.

There was a bleached out, speedy, cocaine vibe to the videos, blasted by lights, grainy, cheap, low budget, but super cool. My favorite VJ was cute virginal Martha Quinn. The videos that most stuck in my mind were:

Men At Work, "Do you cuma from a lann down unda ...
"

White Wedding, Billy Idol, "It's a nice day to start again..."

Michael Jackson, Billie Jean...doot doot...doot doot..."

Billy Joel, Allentown ... "So the graduations hang on the wall. But they never really helped us at all. No, they never taught us what was real. Iron and coke and chromium steel. And we're waiting here in Allentown."

Thomas Dolby, "She Blinded Me with Science".

Heaven 17, "Let Me Go".

Duran Duran, "Her name is Rio ... and she's dancing on the sand."

Haircut 100, "Love Plus One".

Def Leppard, "Photograph". "Oh! Look what you've done to this rock 'n' roll clown! Oh Oh, look what you've done! Photograph - I don't want your ... Photograph - I don't need your ... Photograph - All I've got is a photograph. But it's not enough" I pretended to dislike that one.

Boy George, "Do you really want to hurt me?"

B Movie, "Nowhere Girl ... She's living in a dre-e-am."

Lords Of The New Church, "Open your eyes see the lies right in front of you—Open your eyes!" Boom boom boom boom

Greg Kihn Band, "My Love's in Jeopardy"... Baby ... ooh ooh ooh ooh"

I was a sweet but clueless boyfriend. I had no idea how to be a proper boyfriend. If there was a class I should have taken it. The Blaines had no useful information for me, and my father had zero as well. So I winged it. How did I do?

Here are some statistics.

I never once took her out to dinner or on a nice date.

I didn't want to be alone with her too much. I had fallen too deeply in love ... I mean in need. I always made plans with her and the Blaines on the weekends. I liked hanging out in a group, going to punk shows and being with a bunch of people. She never asked to go on a date so I never took her. Was that a mistake?

Actually, she did ask once. The Culture Club was coming to the Hollywood Palladium. Valerie said she really wanted to go. Their first video, "Do You Really Want to Hurt Me?" was playing on MTV. The Blaines and me were of the firm belief that Culture Club was seriously "wimping."

I shrugged my shoulders and casually said, "I'm not really into it. Just go with Norma."

Was that bad?

The Friday night of Culture Club, Valerie and Norma and I went out for ice cream. Valerie was making it an early night because she had to wake up for a swim meet in the morning. We hung out at her front door for a few moments before she had to go. I didn't want to say goodnight. It felt too early and I hadn't had a good enough dose of her that night. I was starting to feel very worried about losing her.

But, oddly, I seemed to be doing more things than ever to push her away.

She said, "I wish we could spend more time together. I love being with you."

"I do too," I said. "It's usually my fault. I make so many plans with the Blaines."

"Yeah, why?" She smiled, trying to make light of it. "They can be so annoying sometimes."

"We should be together more alone. I don't know why I always make plans with Tim."

"I always end up inviting Norma too. But I can't just forget about her. She's been my best friend since we were babies. I feel like I have to include her. I'd feel too guilty otherwise."

"I thought I was your best friend," I spit out like a big furry baby.

"You're my best friend, too. It's just, Norma ... I have pictures of us playing together in diapers," she smiled in wonder, as she remembered. "But, you know, I was thinking," she said. "Maybe would could go to college together next year and get an apartment?"

"Whoa! ...Where?" I was taken aback.

"Maybe UC Irvine or UC San Diego."

"Irvine? San Diego? UC?" This all of a sudden sounded scary. I probably looked appalled.

"You don't want to?" She looked like I slapped her.

"I'd like to do that ... maybe. Go to college and get an apartment. Irvine sounds kind of weird, and far away. What about UCLA?"

"I probably won't get accepted there," she said. "Also, I want to get away from this place and make a change. I want to get out of this house. I want to get out of the Palisades."

Leaving town, I thought. Leaving the Palisades...that's insane!

But I said, "That might be cool. An apartment, together."

"Yeah."

She gave me a kiss and went inside.

I wasn't expecting to hear what she just said, college somewhere kind of far away? I never even thought of that. Leave the Palisades? Unheard of. I wasn't ready to grow up and leave the Palisades? Hell, I wasn't ready to move out of my parents' house. My mom might freak out if I wasn't around? She'd be more sad and lonely than she already was. I couldn't do it. I wasn't spending much time with my mom anyway and I felt guilty about it. I had to stay close to home.

The band members were getting more and more jealous about me spending so much time with Valerie. Tim, Johnson, and drummer, Adam, were getting more angry and talking a lot of crap together about me as time went on. I wasn't committed enough to the band and hanging out and drinking with them. They would get especially pissed when I would break plans with them to be with Valerie. Here's an example of how they would get back at me passive-aggressive style.

One day after school I decided to buy them some beers in exchange for them hanging out at the beach and shooting super-8 movies of me surfing. The waves were huge and I was excited to get some movies of me surfing. All they had to do was shoot some footage and they got to drink a bunch of beer.

I figured we'd go to our liquor store in Santa Monica where the Asian owners always sold to me even though the birthday on my ID was altered sloppily with Liquid Paper and a pen. I bought a six-pack each of Schlitz Bull Tall's for Tim, Rick and Johnson.

We went to the Sunset Beach and the waves were bigger than they had been in years. The waves were like big, dark-blue, undulating walls, lining up one after the other. The biggest outside sets were about 15 feet, from top to bottom, giant storm surf. That day the swell was washing through million dollar Malibu homes, cleaning them out and turning them into expensive aquariums.

Sunset is the point break at the end of Sunset Blvd near Gladstone's 4 Fish. I could handle Sunset. It's not that steep. The shape was holding up even though it was big. They would roll in instead of dumping top to bottom and walling.

I loaded my camera with film, gave it to Tim, put on my wetsuit and went out to do battle with the big waves. It probably wasn't going to be that fun, but it was so big that if you considered yourself a surfer you had to go out there. This was going to be cool, though, that I was going to get it on film. Tim and Johnson would trade off filming. The beer would keep them occupied and would be a good exchange for their services.

As soon as I started paddling out my board began moving fast sideways southward with the current. The waves were pounding constantly with hardly any breaks between

One Step Beyond

them. I had a half dozen setbacks where big wave sets pushed me back toward the beach and south in the rip tide. Finally after twenty minutes of desperate paddling I got out to past where all but the most enormous waves were breaking. I sat out there far in the ocean. Only the diehard surfers were out. I waved to Tim and Johnson so they would know which guy I was. I saw them wave back.

I felt like a goddamn daredevil out there! I risked my ass on those waves. I caught about ten huge waves and was exhausted. I hoped that they got most of them on film. I was out there for a torturous hour-and-a-half. I had never been so exhausted, paddling constantly to keep from being sucked down the beach, and to keep myself out past most of the big waves. I was just pummeled constantly, though.

I got out of the water and drained my sinuses of seawater as I walked back along the highway. When I got to them I noticed they had finished all the beer and were drunk. Beer cans were strewn all around. I thanked them and told them how much I appreciated them taking the movies. They said they got some excellent footage. I was stoked.

We got in my truck and drove up Sunset Boulevard to go home. Johnson was in the back of the camper with Rick. Tim was up front with me. I looked in my rear-view mirror and couldn't believe what I saw. Johnson had opened up the back of the shell, put down the tailgate, and was lying on his side in the far back peeing out onto Sunset.

It was a big deal too. He did it in front of a dozen people. It was Friday rush-hour traffic. The cars were traveling at about thirty feet apart. The tired-eyed, end-of-the-work-week drivers had no choice but to watch a tall bald nineteen-year-old wag his weenie out the back of my truck and splatter pee off the pavement onto their cars.

"What the fuck!" I said in astonishment to Tim. Tim just smiled, shook his head and shrugged. Johnson had just impressed him.

Johnson had been steadily getting more alcoholic and off the deep end. It seemed that every time he'd drink now he'd pass out or get in a fight or do something terrible. He was a mess. During the past couple punk shows we lost track of him for the whole show and found him later walking around in a daze with a pathetic bloody face. He never could remember what had happened. He had either fallen on his face or got punched or hit in the head with something like a fist, boot or a bottle. The Blaines thought it was funny. He was their personal Sid Vicious. I didn't know what to think or feel about it. I probably felt it was kind of pathetic but just didn't bother doing anything to help him. I didn't feel sorry for him enough. I didn't feel sorry for anyone enough anymore, let alone myself. That would have been a start.

A few days later I got the film back. I was excited as hell to see it. I started up my projector and began to watch. After a couple minutes into the film I realized that this was not a movie about surfing. This was a movie about beer drinking!

They shot a bunch of bumpy drunken footage of themselves hanging out on the rocks chugging whole beers in big single guzzles, burping and heaving the crumpled cans onto the rocks.

Arrrgh!

They got me on one wave, and not a good one. I was pissed but somehow I had to shake my head and laugh. As I

One Step Beyond

watched the final frames of that horrible little movie, I could see that they were wasted and could care even less about surfing than they did in the first place. They had smiles on their faces that said that they were prepared to take my shit after I saw the movie. They thought that was pretty funny. I was starting to get a little tired of these guys.

One Step Beyond
"One Step Beyond" by Madness

Now it was March. I wanted to see more of Valerie but she said she couldn't because she had to go to bed early on Fridays because of swim meets on Saturday mornings. She and her teammates were really dedicated now. They were on their way to city championships. The Palisades' girls' swim team had won city championships five years in a row at this point. They felt the responsibility to keep it going. I was nervous that she was putting distance in there now. She made more plans with the swim team girls on Saturday nights. I asked her if something was wrong; she said everything was okay, and I wanted to believe that.

We all agreed to go see The Exploited (popular punk band from England) play. It was Tim, Norma, Valerie and I. This was another big warehouse concert in Hollywood.

We got there, parked a few blocks away, walked to the front doors and they were closed and they weren't letting any more people in. A couple hundred punks gathered at the entranceway hoping that they would reopen. It was hard for the punkers to believe that the huge warehouse was filled already; it was only 9:30 p.m. We waited there with all the punkers for about a half hour. I was starting to feel claustrophobic at the jam-packed entrance, Tim was determined to stay, and try to get in. I had a sudden urge to get out of there. I told Tim, Norma and Valerie that I had to find a place to pee, that I'd be back soon. I just wanted to get out of there and get some space. I was feeling really rotten, like I was wasting my night and time with Valerie. I'd rather be with her alone. But as usual I didn't grab her and go off with her. I guess I didn't think I could because she had to stay with Norma. Tim told the girls to wait there with him. I was happy to be out of the crowd and was enjoying being alone, taking a look around, people watching. Then I saw some punkers sneaking in through a side door. I decided to run in through the door too. I wandered through the crowds of punks inside. I checked out the scene inside for about fifteen minutes and watched one of the opening bands for a few minutes. Then I realized that I better get back out there and be with them. I exited through the side doors, went around to the front, found the girls and Tim standing in a dispersing crowd of people. Tim was rubbing his eyes angrily, and stomping around yelling, "Jesus!" The girls were crying a little bit and rubbing their eyes.

What happened was the crowd had gotten restless, began pushing and piling themselves up against the door, trying to force the door open to get inside. The police were on the other side of that door, and they opened up just a crack long enough to spray mace in their faces. Tim and the girls were in the line of fire, and got it right in the face.

Right about then, fifty cop cars screeched up to the front of the warehouse. They parked suddenly in a diagonal formation blocking the street. The police stopped the show on the inside and The Exploited never got to play. The police had come to disperse the crowd; they claimed the place was over capacity, but I saw that it was only a quarter full when I was inside.

Punks started yelling at the cops, and then some of them started throwing beer bottles at the cop cars. A bunch of helmeted police officers poured out from inside the warehouse and started chasing the group I was in with their batons swinging in the air. I ran as fast as I could and heard thumps and "uggh" sounds behind me. Blaine and the girls ran in the other direction. I saw Blaine holding the sides of his head as he ran. Then I saw a baton cracking a bald punk right on the head three feet away from me. I felt a swish of a club right by my ear. The guy was aiming for my skull. Shit, I hadn't even done anything wrong. I was just trying to get out of there. I faced forward and ran the hell out of there. My heart was racing. I was now a few blocks away and pretty much in the clear. I was trembling and so relieved that I didn't get hit. I was scared and felt like finding a spot to hide for a while, but I kept going. Other punks were breaking windows in the buildings and storefronts as I jogged down the street. I didn't want to be associated with that. I wasn't sure where my truck was. I was disoriented and didn't know what direction to go and it took me about twenty minutes to find it.

When I got back to the truck, Valerie, Tim and Norma were waiting for me. They were standing on the curb, rubbing their sore, stingy eyes. The girls were mad that I left them earlier and had taken so long to get back to the truck. Tim was angry about being maced. I think he kind of liked it, actually; it was exciting and provided another good war story. The girls were obviously shaken from being maced, and didn't like it. Nobody said anything as we drove home. I didn't know what to say to comfort them. I only said that it was a fucked situation and I was sorry it happened, and then I just stayed quiet. The girls were whimpering a bit on the way home; they were traumatized by it. I wondered how bad it was to be maced. I figured it probably was worse than I thought. Every now and then I'd hear a blurting sob come out of them. I felt sorry for them and guilty for leaving them. But that's how I always had been. I was so used to going off on my own.

I tried making plans with Valerie for the next weekend. No luck. Friday she said she had to go to bed early because of the swim meet and on Saturday she had plans with her friends. I had the bad feeling she was pulling away. I didn't know what she was thinking. I talked to her on the phone only briefly in the past week and she seemed cool and short with me. I asked her what was up but she wouldn't tell me. It felt like she was getting more detached from me. I was starting to feel desperate and sad. She wouldn't tell me what was going on with her. I made plans with the guys to try to forget about it for now. I wanted to just do some drinking. Like on TV with relationship problems.

On Friday I went to San Gabriel with Tim and practiced with the band. We drank about a case of beer while practicing. Then on Saturday night I went out drinking with Tim and Johnson. I drove to the liquor store in Santa Monica. I bought a whole case of Schlitz Bull malt liquor talls for the three of us.

I drove with Tim and Johnson up to the top of a street in the Palisades where there was a beautiful view. We sat there staring at the view while "pounding" the beers. We talked about punk and people we knew and more punk and things that annoyed us, which was everything, and all the usual stuff. Three big punk gossips. I tried not to talk about Valerie too much with Tim and Johnson, even though I wanted to desperately. They didn't want to hear it. Whenever I tried to talk about it they changed the subject. I forced it all inside, though it was all I could think about. I figured that they were probably jealous and angry with the subject of "me and my girlfriend," because there was no subject of "them and their girlfriends." Instead we talked about the band and our plans to play an upcoming gig at Loyola High School's talent show. Adam, our drummer, went to Loyola, a private Catholic all-guys high school that we called Boyola.

Little did we realize, while gabbing away, we drank the whole case! I guess I wasn't paying much attention, because drinking the whole case of beer was not a good idea.

We didn't think too hard about the fact that we drank eight 16-ounce malt liquor beers each in two hours—with no dinner. And what do three teenagers do after drinking that much beer in so little time?

Throw up, that's right. Or pass out, or both. Or do what Johnson did.

Blaine and I didn't throw up for some reason, but we did pass out. We passed out while still sitting upright in the cab of my truck. Johnson was in the bed of the truck like a caged animal, which was enclosed by the fiberglass shell. For him to speak with us he would have to stick his head up in the frame of the little sliding window. It was an uncomfortable little place with only a dirty carpet back there for him.

Anyway he left his den while we were asleep, and he went off to pillage and destroy.

Pillage and destroy what?

We didn't know yet, and we wouldn't find out until the next morning. All I could remember from that night after we drank the beer was the following conversation.

I heard Johnson yelling, "Hey, we gotta get out of here! Now! We gotta go, man...hurry!"

He was on low volume, though, the station wasn't coming in clear because I was too groggy and sleepy. I was starting to come around a little bit.

I mumbled, "Wha...?"

"Let's go ... Come on, man! Let's go!" He said.

"But why?" I asked him, "I'm tired. I can't see..."

I finally sat up and was horrified to see that all my vision was rolling upward at a thousand-frames-per-second. I vaguely, blurredly, saw Johnson to my right in the little window yelling and pushing me back and forth. The scenery was flying upwards frantically fast. I had the spins. But these were not the usual horizontal ones; these were vertical.

I told Johnson, "I can't drive. I can't even see. Why? Why do we have to go?"

The last thing he said was, "Put it this way, man, if we don't leave now, we're going to get busted by the cops—so ... LET'S GO!"

"Okay. If you put it that way."

I peeled the hell out of there. And I don't remember anything else...until I woke up the next morning. Blaine was on the floor next to me and I was in my bed, it was 12:30 p.m. We had the worst hangovers ever and my head throbbed horribly. He got off the floor and I got out of bed. We could barely walk, bent over, both of us with gigantic, pulsating

One Step Beyond

headaches, poisoned by alcohol. With every step we took it was like pounding nails into our brains. We both felt like we were on the verge of barfing every second.

Then we looked at each other at the same time, thinking, "Oh, my God! Where's Johnson?" We tried thinking, but it hurt too much. We couldn't figure it out. We hobbled out my front door, down my front steps, and out to the garage to where my truck was. I was glad my mom wasn't around to see us. I'm sure we looked ghastly.

I just wanted to possibly figure out where Johnson was, take Tim home, and go back to bed. I looked at my truck, baffled that it seemed to be sitting there in one piece. I walked around it, circling it, slowly, dizzily, surveying it, my head pounding and pounding.

Uh oh. My front fender was smashed, completely crunched in. My headache immediately got worse. I was sweating and my heart was beating along with my head. I looked for signs of somebody else's paint on top of my paint, which would tell me that I hit a parked car.

Then the thought hit me, "No, not a moving car?"

I found wood chips. Thank God! I must of hit a pole or fence; it was probably a telephone pole judging by the color.

I felt bad, sick and disturbed, because I'd never crashed my car before. Was I irresponsible? Was I out of control? Was there something seriously wrong with me?

Then I got pissed and started blaming others, because that's always easier.

"Johnson," I said. "That asshole! What was that all about last night!"

I walked around to the back of my truck and lifted the shell window, and then the pieces of the big, ugly puzzle all started to fall into place. The back of my truck was filled with all kinds of crap: patio furniture, potted plants, non-potted plants, mailboxes, anything people decorate their patios and backyards with, a ton of miscellaneous stuff. Johnson, in a crazed raid, had looted whatever he could pull off of the side of houses, gardens, back yards, front yards, and he had thrown it all into the back of my truck.

While we were passed out, he went on a giant spree. He had gone from house to house and removed anything and everything that wasn't nailed down. He then threw it all into the back of my truck and went and got more.

There were seat cushions, barbeque tops, bird feeder, a hose, firewood, wall lanterns. Etc.

We were shocked. Someone we knew could be that nuts? We sifted through the stuff in disbelief. And then we found Johnson.

He arose, groggily, up from the debris, as if from an excavation, an archaeological find! Johnson was resurrected from the shit heap. He had buried himself underneath all the junk, and pulled it over him the night before like it was a blanket.

One Step Beyond

He couldn't even get up so we left him in the shit heap. Then we drove to the park, where they had a dumpster, and he got out and we took turns heaving the crap into the dumpster and hurling barf onto the grass. Baby-carriage-cruising Sunday yupsters looked at us, like something was wrong. They were right; something was wrong. Very wrong.

"HuuHHGG!" onto the grass.

Something had to change. It was obvious. I knew it. Johnson knew it. Tim didn't know it, though.

Johnson went to AA right after that. He hit bottom that night. I figured I probably needed to get my shit together too. I didn't think my drinking was out of control but my life was. I knew I was on a bad path. Down a wrong road that headed into poles.

This disturbed me: I crashed my truck without knowing it. That is not good. I should have been more worried about getting maimed or killed in some kind of stupid accident.

Johnson may have learned the most from this incident.

He got himself a job at the transcendental meditation center as a gardener. He grew his hair out to a normal length and lived a mellow lifestyle for a long time.

This was good. He became very mellow. This was very good.

The next day I went to Valerie's and told her about what had happened and she just looked at me with a puzzled look, like I was funny. She smiled and shook her head in amazement. I could say that she minimized it, but I did too, and she might have taken my lead or just been so over me anyway. I told the story in a funny way that made it easier to make light of. I didn't want to take it seriously. It was easier to laugh at it. I rationalized, Hey, nothing horrible happened.

Our band had our biggest show coming up. I threw myself into getting ready for that. It was a big show with other bands at Loyola boy's high school. First we had to audition and get the gig. Then we could rehearse and get ready for our assault on their school.

Mike Pearson

The Fat Lady Sings, Live At Boyola

"Do You Really Want to Hurt Me" by Culture Club

Johnson was in rehab. There would be no more singing punk rock for him. It was 12-step time. We asked him to sing but he said he couldn't sing unless he was drunk. He needed to be wasted to lose his inhibitions and go wild. I think he also knew it was good to stay away from the Blaines' horrible influence. Fortunately, Tim knew a guy who could replace Johnson. Ron Bane. Ron was the first singer of Violent Attack, the singer before Johnson. He already knew most of the songs. He and Tim had had a falling out a year earlier. Tim had pressured him to spend more time with him and the band, but Bane's first love was water polo. He agreed to do this show for us. He was a great punk singer; he had a good solid voice and style. His style ranged from super intense to funny and goofy and bizarre at times. I wished that he would join the band but that wasn't going to happen. I don't think he liked Tim trying to control him. He never made it big at water polo, but a few years later he joined the FBI. He was a real eccentric.

We went to Boyola one afternoon to audition for the show. We set up our equipment in the middle of the gym, and did three songs for the adult talent show committee. We had to give them a different name too, something less threatening.

Violent Attack wasn't going to fly—it made us sound like terrorists, so we told them we were Happy Road Kill. We couldn't stop laughing when we came up with that one. We put on button down shirts for the audition, trying to look as normal as possible, even though our hair was short and dyed funny colors. Adam had black hair, Tim had white, and I had white hair with black tips. I looked like a skunk.

We had planned on slowing our songs down and playing mellower for the audition but we just couldn't control ourselves. We played at our normal frantic break-neck hardcore speed. I remember thinking that we must've looked like maniacs in front of the conservative Catholic committee. I thought there was no way they'd let us play. But they picked us. We couldn't understand why they would let us play? Adam asked one of the committee members and she said the reason was because they thought it would be good to have a little diversity in the line-up, because so far every band that auditioned was a similar '80s New Wave cover band.

We saw the other bands auditioning. One of the bands played The Pretender's "Back on the Chain Gang." Then another band came on looking just like that one and they played "Promises, Promises" by Naked Eyes. Then there were some people who smiled way too much and played Bow Wow Wow's "I Want Candy" with so much enthusiasm that they broke out in a real mean sweat and were huffing and puffing afterwards. Then there were some other people who couldn't decide whether they were new wave or Fleetwood Mac. Then there was us.

Finally the night of the show came. Valerie and Norma said they were coming and driving separately and meeting us there. We hung out with our friends and watched the first

One Step Beyond

couple bands. More and more of our friends started showing up. We noticed that a whole bunch of punks were showing up whom we didn't even know. These couldn't all be Boyola punkers? We had promoted the show by putting flyers in record stores and telling everyone we knew. Word had caught on in the punk community that this would be a good punk show. I knew that this was going to be our best show ever. At 10 p.m. we started to set up. I was up on stage, plugging everything in, looking at the whole dance hall, and it was packed with people. There must have been about 600 or 700 people there. We definitely had the best slot. We were set to go on at 10:30 p.m., the peak hour. I was excited. This was going to be great. There was a lot of energy in the air. We sound checked for a few bars. We were ready. A kid we knew, Chunky Monkey, hopped onto the stage and gave us a cute introduction. "Gentlemen and gentlemen, give a warm welcome to ... VIOLENT ATTACK!"

We launched into our opener, a fast, powerful punk version of the Mission Impossible theme song, complete with the note-for-note guitar part, but shrieking with loud distortion. Ronald Bane jumped onto stage and grabbed the microphone.

The slam pit started whirling into action and was getting bigger and wilder by the second. By our second song, "Fucked Up Ronnie," a D.O.A. song about Reagan, the place was going completely nuts. There was a huge slam pit! Ron Bane introduced our third song by throwing out an insulting comment to the Dean of Students in the form of a dedication.

"This song is dedicated to Dean McMurphy. It's called N-N-H." Then he said, "NEHHH!"—Like an animal, grunting. "It stands for Nowhere Near Human. It's about certain creatures who have their heads misdirected so far up a certain area of their anatomy that they can't see or understand shit!"

Adam clicked off the sticks. 1-2-3-4. And we launched into N.N.H. Adam was nervous about getting in trouble in school (he was actually a really good student) so he started his drumstick count-off as fast as he could, attempting to cover up the "shit".

During the third song, people started stage diving at Catholic high school. I couldn't believe it. That was the best. There were punks everywhere. It turned out really wild and great.

We did eighteen songs in forty minutes with only the machinegun clik-clik-clik-clik of the drumsticks in between to cue us in. The slam pit was big, about fifty feet in diameter. The whole place was churning.

One Step Beyond

At the end of our set, I looked behind me and saw Tim throwing his guitar about ten feet in the air and catching it over and over again. Adam was kicking his drum set all around and into pieces.

I had no idea they were going to do that. I looked at my bass, and it was brand new, so I decided to put it down and join in kicking Adam's drum set around. Then we hopped off the stage and mingled and partied with the people. It was the best show we had ever had by far.

We got an awesome response from the audience. We didn't win the talent prize, though. The people who liked us would never be caught dead filling out a talent show ballot. The band that played Bow Wow Wow won because their fans were exactly the type of people who would be caught dead filling them out.

I got a bad feeling from Valerie, though. I saw her in the audience with Norma while I was playing. She had her arms crossed and a detached look on her face as she watched us. She seemed cold.

Afterwards, I approached her but she stayed close to Norma and acted like she was always busy talking to her or someone else. When I tried talking to her, she made it a point not to respond much and just kept turning away to Norma and walking off somewhere with her to chat. I was so taken aback I didn't know what to do. I didn't have the nerve to simply say, "Hey, what the hell is going on? Let's talk." She said she had to go. I hung out with a bunch of punks after the show.

The next day and a few days after that I called her but her family said she wasn't there. I became desperate and distraught and I asked Tim about it.

One Step Beyond

He replied, "Dude, Valerie says you're way too negative and she can't handle it anymore."

"She told you this?"

"You gotta admit ... you're way negative, dude. She's got sick of hearing it."

"What have you heard?" I asked.

"She just said, man, you're always negative and she's sick of it, because she said, no matter what, you're never happy."

"That's not true. I'm happy," as I began to cry.

"Man, I'm just telling you what she said. It is true, man. You complain a lot. A lot of guys would be stoked to have Valerie, but you don't appreciate her."

By the next Friday night I couldn't stand it anymore. I went over to her house to confront her. I went over feeling kind of hopeful, thinking that I might be able to get Friday night plans with her. I was way wrong. Then she gave me the famous line: "I don't feel like being in a relationship with you, or anyone, at this time." My heart was breaking. It was beating fast, then it felt like it cracked into a million pieces. I just stood there dumbfounded. "What? What are you talking about?"

She repeated basically the same thing a few more times.

Then I asked, "Well, do you think you might want to get back together later?"

"I don't know. I don't know how I feel. Maybe ... But not for a while. I don't know. I can't say right now. I just need a break."

So I left, feeling sick and depressed. I went home and got dressed to go to a Pali High dance by myself. The popular Santa Monica mod band Eight Ball was playing. Everybody in town was going. I went hoping that I could talk to her and that she would have a change of heart. Maybe I would have a chance to patch it up. At the dance she avoided me; she stayed interlocked with Norma, arm in arm, and turned the other way like she didn't see me when I approached them. I felt pathetic. I would have been better off if I was angry at her. I just felt sad and dejected. I was too passive and defeated to be assertive and try to make her talk to me. She just avoided me and I let her. I thought that we might be able to talk it out. But she wanted to move on, immediately. I was supposed to go along with being eliminated, so I did.

I was wounded. The next few days I cried and cried. I had never felt so depressed and lonely. All my old unworthiness, abandonment and neglect feelings were dredged up. The hardcore toxins that had been laying underneath my emotional crust was unearthed now. I had a million pathetic thoughts like, "How could she have ever loved me if she wouldn't even take the time with me to talk about this? I felt disposable. I didn't know about my family issues at the time (pre-therapy), so I figured that it was all about this abandonment and neglect, all about Valerie. I felt like a super victimized loser. Most of my emotions had been suppressed since I was a kid. Now my emotions were flooding out, but I didn't know how to support myself during this. My defenses had been blown apart. A big problem was that I didn't have friends to turn to. I had let my mod friends go mostly; plus, I had never become that close with any of them anyway. All I had was the Blaines. And the Blaines weren't capable of being supportive. So I was screwed.

One Step Beyond

The concert was such a high point; the show was awesome. Then immediately I dipped into one of the lowest points of my life.

The day after the breakup I was at the Blaines' and I lay down on their dirty living room carpet and started to cry. Tim saw me and didn't know what to do. He didn't have any empathy and he just said, "Dude, you're wimping. Sob story!" Minor Threat just came out with an album that had a song on it called Sob Story, so he started singing that to me.

"Life's not been good for you—It's just not fair

You did nothing to deserve it—You did nothing at all.

Sit back and watch - It turns from bad to worse.

No matter how loud you cry - It always hurts

Then the chorus:

Boy, I'm glad, I'm not in your shoes

How could things get any worse for you

You're so fucking alone

How could things get any worse for you?"

Then I decided I better pull it together and toughened up. I got up off the floor, and wiped my eyes. Then I decided to confront him about the band. I'd wanted to confront him for a while about taking the band more seriously.

I said, "Tim, if we are going to do the band I think we should try to take it to the next level. We're always playing parties when we could be playing big punk shows with big bands. A lot of other bands are doing it and are not as good as us. I think we should get it together for real and tour with bands and make an album. If we're going to do it we need to get serious and find a new singer."

Tim said, "Bane only cares about water polo. He's a sell-out yuppie."

"We can do this for real," I said. "The other night at Boyola proved that. We have good songs and we're a good band. We need to put in more effort, and set up real shows. We can do it. We've been selling ourselves short."

"I know. The songs are killer, but I don't want to do it, because Johnson should be singing. I don't want to do the band unless Johnson's singing."

"That's bullshit, man. We can get someone else. He can't even sing while sober."

"He's the best singer and the only one. I'm not doing it without Johnson! It doesn't matter, anyway, man. Adam's not going to be around. He got accepted at Santa Cruz; he's gone, the fuckin' hippie. He's the best drummer, and the only drummer for this band!"

"Give me a fuckin' break! We can find another drummer and singer."

I knew it was time to quit arguing with him. I knew that he was afraid of trying and failing. It was safer to not to try and pretend he could have done it if he had wanted to. If he did try, and he failed, then his dad was right, he was a loser.

That weekend I went to our last band practice in San Gabriel. After an aimless, gutless practice, Tim, Adam and I went to a Kentucky Fried Chicken on a super wide and ugly boulevard. It was 100 degrees out and it had that hot asphalt valley heat, dry, with no air movement. It was cold and well air-conditioned in the KFC.

I hadn't talked to Adam about the Valerie situation yet. I wanted to see if he had anything kind for me. For instance, "Fuck that bitch, there are plenty of other girls," would have been helpful. There was no response. They both just sat there expressionless while fidgeting with their food and slurping their Orange Bangs. I was hoping for something, a little support. Tim blurted out, "Wimping," between chews of his chicken. He was showing off to Adam. "Sob Story," Tim spurted out, while chewing. Then he added, "wimping" again with his hand over his mouth, as if he was clearing something that was stuck in his throat. Adam had a smirk on his face like he was supposed to.

So that was it with the band. Done. I couldn't be with them anymore.

Two weeks later there was a family party at Valerie's house for her sister's ninth-grade graduation. Her sister had called me and said she wanted me to come; I had become close with her over the last six months. I went to the party and said goodbye to her sister and brother and mom and dad. At the party Valerie and Norma and all the swim-team girlfriends ignored me like I was diseased.

Mike Pearson

One Step Beyond

The Beards
"I've Had It" by Black Flag

I dropped by the Blaines' house one last time. I gave a haircut to a kid, got a haircut, saw a snake eat a rat and watched Ronnie blow up a mailbox that he stole from someone's house. That night I went to my final punk show with the Blaines. It was Tim, Rick, and myself. D.O.A. from Canada, was playing at Club Lingerie in Hollywood. Club Lingerie was a 21 and over club.

We were excited to see D.O.A. They were one of the best punk bands. The Blaines had a problem with their fake IDs, though—they were too fake. They had cut tiny square holes in their old-style, non-laminated, California IDs, where their birth dates were, and they inserted new numbers from other IDs in the old holes they cut out. If you took it out of the scratched opaque plastic window in the wallet you would instantly see that it was fake.

They needed some way to get in to the show, some way to make the doorman think they were old enough. I looked older and had a fake ID that looked fairly real so I wasn't worried about it.

I went to their house at 7 p.m. and found them working away at something in the garage. They were making beards and applying them to their faces. They were convinced these beards would get them into the show. They said it had worked before.

Rick had his on, but he hadn't trimmed it yet, and it looked disgusting. It consisted of clumps of gray and brown hair, and it looked dirty.

They said not to worry; it wasn't finished.

Rick had the contact cement out, and he was about to apply a bunch of beard hair, which he had in a brown paper lunch bag. I told him I thought that contact cement was overkill, and that he could use something else, like white glue, and he told me, "When you do beards you have to go all the way, man ... That shit sticks like crazy!" He said that was what they used the last time.

So where did the dirty-looking hair come from? My question was answered when I saw the dog come walking around the corner with a big bald patch of hair missing on its butt. They shaved their dog's ass with the buzzer, level zero. His butt was now nothing but a pink irritated bald dog's ass. The filthy hair was in the bag waiting to be applied.

Rick took out some big hunks and began to patch them onto Tim's face.

I asked, "What are you going to do about the color of that gray-brown dog-colored shit?"

They assured me they had it all worked out. After applying the hair, they pulled out a couple black permanent markers and took turns coloring in each other's faces.

At that point, I went home and ate. Two hours later, I returned to pick them up. I pulled into the driveway, and two short, young, dark-bearded men walked out of the front door.

One Step Beyond

Their mom appeared in the doorway, smiling and waving goodbye to them.

"Bye, boys, have a good time," their mom yelled, smiling. She understood. She knew how they loved that "Dead on Arrival."

We drove up Sunset Boulevard to the club. We parked down the street and walked up to the front door.

"Sorry, guys, I need IDs," the doorman spat out instantly. The boys immediately began to explain how they had just forgot them. They used voices that were a lot lower than normal.

"Uh, yeah," Tim said, seriously, gruffly. "I don't know what happened. We must've left 'em at the house."

One Step Beyond

The doorman stuck to his guns.

"Sorry, guys can't do it. I need IDs."

"Oh, man. I can't believe this!" Tim said, to the doorman.

Rick said, "What? No way!" and stomped a boot to the ground.

And their beards were so thick, too.

They couldn't believe it didn't work. They were pissed.

I would have been surprised if it did work. Then Rick said to me, "Come on, man, let's go around to the back door and try bribing somebody to let us in."

I figured okay, and we walked around to the back. Rick and Tim wanted me to knock on the back door and do the bribing. No problem. They gave me $5 each.

I knocked on the back door and a tall Hollywood doorman, tattooed, in his mid-thirties answered. I said, "Hey, my friends forgot their IDs, and D.O.A. is their favorite band. Could I give you some cash to do us this favor? I pulled out $20.

He looked around, checking for anyone watching, and then asked me quickly in a hushed tone, "Where are the guys?"

I hesitated for a second, then I said, "Well ... they have beards—"

"Those two guys?! I can't let them in!"

Then he wanted me to tell him the whole story about the beards. I told him the story and he was very amused, but he still was unwilling to let them in.

I told the Blaines that they weren't going to get in. I began walking out of the alley, heading down the sidewalk, toward my truck. They followed behind me. They were pressuring me, bugging me. Rick pleaded, "Let's go back and talk to him again. Come on, man. Let's see if he'll take more money?"

"Let's give him an extra five bucks," Tim said.

"He'll do it! Let's try," Rick said. "Then we'll try it with the guy in the front, Tim said."

"Yeah," Rick said.

"Just one more try," Tim said.

I turned around and stopped in front of them. They both came to a halt and looked at me seriously for a moment.

"Come on, Mike," they both pleaded.

"No," I said. "We're going home."

One Step Beyond

Afterward
"End of the Party" by The English Beat

I was done with the Blaines. I didn't know who to hang out with. There weren't many mods left. That group was falling apart, a lot of them had coupled off. A few of my gas station buddies were still around, but I didn't feel like hanging out with them. I spent most of my time with some young punkers, taking them to shows during spring and through the summer. That was fun at times (we went to some great shows), but a lot of the time I was just depressed. It's wild how teenagers still have energy even when they are depressed. I remember feeling irritable, angry, hopeless, and just wanting to be alone but not liking that either.

The best thing that happened was that I formed a new band. The band lasted almost five years and we had a great time. We played many local parties, but we never broke out beyond that. Boney sang and played guitar, and we got John from the gas station to play rhythm guitar at times. My brother's friend played drums. A lot of times we rocked out with a goofy '80s drum machine. It sounded oddly powerful and was hilarious at the same time. The Red Hot Chili Peppers had come out recently, and we loved them, so we were a bit like them. But we were more disco than funk, and more Devo than punk.

Mike Pearson

One of our cool gigs was up in the mountains above the Palisades at a spot called Skull Rock. Skull Rock was an awesome place, a big skull-shaped rock formation on the top of a mountain that was perched overlooking a deep canyon. A 15-year kid organized the whole thing. He got a generator and kegs. There were about five bands that started at sunset and went into the night. The kid got a Black Flag offshoot band called Würm to play. Würm had Black Flag's great rhythm section, Chuck Dukowski and Bill Stevenson. Two other bands were from the Palisades. One was fourteen year olds (my brother's friends), and another was a progressive jazzy punk band with fifteen year olds. The bands were great for how young they were. They had all original songs. The fifth band was a tough punk band from Mar Vista, Neighborhood Watch. We drove our trucks up the newly graded mountain at the top of Palisades Drive. There were acres of bulldozed treeless land. They were going to build multi-million-dollar tract home mansions in a few months. It had been beautiful there in the hills. We would see hawks soaring around. We would sometimes spend the night up there, either up on the flattened top of a giant rock near the skull, or, during the chilly months, we'd sleep inside the shallow cave right below. Coyotes would yip and squeal throughout the night. Skull Rock used to seem so far away from civilization; that was before they leveled the surrounding area to build. Soon there would be a big box mansion right next to Skull. Yuck! The mansions would be built as large as possible (4000 or 5000 square feet) with only about fifteen feet for a backyard. This was the beginning of builders doing this.

We were sitting around throwing out band names when we came up with the name for our new band. Bat & Lizard. For some reason we couldn't stop laughing. I don't know

One Step Beyond

why we thought it was so funny. I guess we were already delirious from thinking up funny names. We had ones that were a bit too crude: Butt Foam, Split Sack, Penis in Pieces, Hanging Stool.

Ones that were too stupid and silly: Baby Internaciönal, Chicks into Rush, Mote Dungeon, Cauldron, Child Slayer, Sodomy, Battle Cry, Snake Breath, Ümläut Frënzy and We Now Have Sex With Each Other Because Our Girlfriends Have Bailed Us.

We settled on Bat & Lizard.

Boney would introduce himself as Bat, and I as Lizard. We even had a call and response theme song that we would start out with each time, where we would scream out our names as the chorus.

"BAT!!" - "LIZARD!!"

I would step on a digital delay foot pedal that would repeat the names with a psycho echo.

We drove up to the mountains in my four-wheel drive. We got out, greeted everyone, started drinking beer and unloading our equipment. As the sun went down, Shower of Smegma played, and after them Magnolia Thunderpussy. About fifty or sixty punks showed up. We provoked the overly serious punkers by playing out-of-style '70s hesher rock but with a super fast punk beat. I dressed up like a hippie gypsy woman, a ridiculous cross between Stevie Nicks and the You Spin Me Right Round Baby guy. Boney wore a black denim jacket and had his hair greased back; he was going for the Frankie Goes to Hollywood look. Our 2nd guitarist dressed up like the guy from the band Boston, a 1970s studio musician with a big Jewish fro and giant glasses. We looked so funny in our outfits. People were staring at us, confused and probably thinking that the wrong band had showed up, but we acted like we were dead serious and played really fast and hard for all the punkers on the mountain. We opened with a super speed version of Deep Purple's Highway Star, the grueling classic metal song about a man's love for his car.

We played all our songs straight-faced, and it took a couple songs before the kids understood what we were doing and started slamming and enjoying it. I saw Chuck Dukowski leaning up against his truck; he was drinking beer and headbanging to us.

One Step Beyond

Dukowski was kind of rocking out to us and this made me feel awesome. I loved that guy; he was my favorite punk bassist. He would often warm up before Black Flag would play. He was like an opening act, playing by himself, building up intensity, playing loud and powerfully, getting himself and others psyched for Black Flag.

We had a great time playing that night at Skull. I always forgot my problems when playing music or going surfing. Around this time I got more into surfing. I would go a few times a week. This helped relieve my anxiety and sadness and made me feel more free of emotional pain. It was a distraction and it postponed me having to really feel my underlying feelings, but it provided some relief. I went to Malibu point almost every day. I couldn't ruminate on how miserable I was when I was focused on catching and riding waves.

A month into summer I met some new guys and girls. We hung out and drank a lot and partied together and dove and swam in a Santa Monica Canyon park pool at night. We listened to KROQ music like Tears for Fears and goofed around dancing ironically to Safety Dance (I guess that's the only way you can dance to Men Without Hats). We went to some awesome punk shows that summer, like Siouxsie & the Banshees and Black Flag at the Santa Monica Civic, Minor Threat, and many great smaller shows like SS Decontrol from Boston. I was friends with a 14 year old girl and she would climb up on my shoulders and we would chicken fight at all the shows. We would take mushrooms and I would dive into the shallow five-foot-deep park pool in the middle of the night. We hung out until all hours of the night, drinking beer, on a secluded staircase that descended from a quiet neighborhood that overlooked the ocean a block north of

One Step Beyond

Sunset Blvd. We had many super deep conservations that I would love to hear a recording of now to see how deep they really were.

The school year started and I decided to focus more on school and do more homework. I kept to myself more. I was looking forward to going to a four-year college.

Around this time I read in the paper (and heard through friends) that the Blaines were at a party spot in the Palisades when a 13-year-old boy, who was with them, was shot and killed. The story went that somebody in the group had provoked an angry drifter who lived in a motor home near where they were partying by yelling insults at him. He came out with a shotgun, aimed, shot and fired, and hit and killed the boy. When I heard this I was sad for the boy and his family but also so relieved that I had stopped hanging around with them. I thought that that could have been me. I felt lucky to have been through all I had been through and still be okay.

Some harsh things happened over the next couple of years, though. People were dying here and there from being reckless. A 16-year-old girl who I had dated was killed in a car accident while with her new boyfriend. The next year a girl, who my friends and I used to drive around drinking with, was killed, when her friend, drove into a telephone pole at high speed while coming down a steep hill. Weekend after weekend we used to drive all over town, going from party to party, sipping off a big bottle of vodka. At least half a dozen kids from the Palisades were killed in car accidents while driving high or drunk in the 80s. A popular girl was raped and murdered by a security guard in a retail office building in town.

In 1984 I started doing cocaine. I started out buying a little (a quarter gram) with a friend. After a couple of months my friend and I were buying a gram together, then two. After three months of this I started worrying that I had become addicted. I was doing coke almost daily now. It was making me more depressed too, when I would come down. After about six months of this it all culminated with my friend getting severely beaten in an alley while buying coke. He was hospitalized and had to have a rod put in his cheek to stabilize it. This scared the hell out of me and I stopped cold turkey. I decided to stay home with my parents and chill. This went on for about six months. Many of my high school friends were drinking nightly together. I hung out with my parents, sober, watching TV with them at night. I got more involved in school and began to get A's and was ready to transfer to a four-year college. I stayed mostly sober after this, except for getting a little drunk at parties here and there.

Finally at age 22 I met a really nice, sweet girl and fell in love and had my best relationship yet. It was what I was hoping and waiting for for so long. I was able to be myself with her and I let my guard down, and she could do the same. We went out for four years and I was mostly happy during this time. This was a very healing relationship for me.

After being with her for about a year I had some more losses. In 1988 my dad and childhood dog, Buddy, and good friend and brother's girlfriend, all died within a six month time period. These deaths sent me back into a moderate depression. My girlfriend moved away to college in 1991. This loss opened up my old wound. My lonely-guy, empty, neglect issues got activated again. She broke up with me on my 27th birthday. I had just moved into a new apartment, and I didn't even have sheets on my bed yet when she came over

One Step Beyond

and told me we were done. I thought we were going to go out that night. She had met her new boyfriend at college; he lived in her dorm. That birthday night I went to sleep on a bed without sheets with boxes all around and nothing unpacked. I felt totally insane.

The '90s had begun and the first half absolutely sucked. Nothing seemed fun. Dull and dreary. I isolated myself and didn't like being with people. I didn't want to go out drinking with old friends. I didn't have any new friends. The positive side was that I was sober and not getting into trouble. After my dad died, I inherited some money from my grandfather who I never knew, and got into buying old houses and fixing them up and selling them. I also was a real estate loan broker for a while. I played some music with Boney. We had a duo, then later a trio, where we played acoustic folk, lounge, hillbilly and roots music. It was pretty wimpy but it was something to do. I couldn't get him to rock. He was in an anti-rock mood. He soon got into jazz. I then joined a hard rock band, sort of grungy with a trippy keyboard. That blew up after a few months due to the band members' drug addiction and serious lack of self-esteem.

I realized that I needed to become more social again. I had sheltered myself from 1991 to 1995, all through my late 20s. Boney suggested that I work with him at the Los Angeles Music Center as an usher. The pay was ridiculous, but it was fun and I quickly met dozens of people. I remembered that I was actually a social person. I got to see good plays, musicals, the opera and the L.A. Philharmonic. The Music Center consisted of the Dorothy Chandler Pavilion (opera and orchestra), Mark Taper Forum (small theater), and the Ahmanson Theater (bigger theater and musicals).

I soon met a new girlfriend. For a variety of reasons, too annoying to go into, the relationship ended six months later with a deafening OWW. It dawned on me that I didn't know what the hell I was doing regarding relationships. Something was really out of whack with my choices in women and how I would relate to them (caretaking them like a desperate codependent monkey). This finally sent me into therapy. My goal upon entering therapy was to resolve all my issues and problems within six months. I was really concerned and pissed off when I realized that, after a year, that I had just barely gotten started healing and understanding myself. Four years later, in 2000, I had gotten so much out of therapy (and appreciated and liked it so much so) that I decided to go back to school and get my therapist license so I could help others the way I was helped. I was feeling a thousand times better. I was now "okay" and could help others. I could now come from a place of abundance instead of some weird unhealthy vicarious place.

I needed to get my hours toward my license (3000 total) and I wanted to get paid at the same time, so I got a job working with severely emotionally disturbed teenagers at a locked inpatient acute psychiatric treatment facility. I didn't think I would like love it (I wanted to work with more verbal adults), but I was happy to get my hours quickly and get paid. Then I started to really enjoy it. The facility is basically a big psych hospital/group home with a non-public school on premise. It's at an old hospital that was converted. It's home to 50 kids who get treatment for depression, severe mood swings, suicidality, danger-to-self behaviors, danger-to-others behavior, fighting and all kinds of acting out and substance abuse. There are equal amounts of blacks, whites and Hispanics. No Asians for some reason. The kids stay there about for about 6 months to 3 or 4 years depending on how severe they are. These kids were taken out of their homes (often when very young) by the Department of Children and Family Services. Most of them were removed due to severe abuse and neglect. Some of them had too many problems due to the effects of early neglect and prenatal substance abuse and their family (bio, relatives or adoptive parents) weren't able to manage them. Many of them have lived at 15 to 20 placements (foster homes, group homes, etc). About 2/3rds of them have no viable family members to take them in. These kids have not been successful at less restrictive settings, foster homes, six bed group-homes, bigger Level 12 group homes (which are unlocked), and ultimately they end up at our facility which is the highest level of care available: an acute psych hospital and a locked CTF Community Treatment Facility.

These kids are the most traumatized that California has to offer. Many of the kids get frustrated and upset when they were at an unlocked placement, they don't feel safe, and they run away (searching for something, often unconsciously looking for something like "mommy" or "daddy") and they get themselves in various degrees of trouble and end up in juvenile hall or a psych hospital. Some of them have brain issues from neglect, prenatal substance exposure, and genetic mental illness that runs in the family. 95% of our girls have been sexually abused, most often by stepfathers. The kids are referred to us because of suicidal ideation, attempts, "cutting" and other self harm and self destructive behavior, like running away and prostituting. They are used to being hurt and they reenact their traumas (sexual abuse, physical abuse, abandonment, etc) repeatedly.

The kids go to school until 2:30 p.m., and then they do therapeutic groups until 8:30 at night. They all have individual and group therapy. After a year or two of getting their needs met (catching up emotionally and developmentally) and healing wounds and learning to cope adequately enough to be able to live in the world, they move to a lower level of care and sometimes home—if there is a home.

It's very fulfilling to help them. I started as a group therapist and then became a primary therapist, and then Admissions Director. I'm the one who brings all the kids in. They are often referred by social workers. (Hell, I would have brought my own 14-year-old ass in if I weren't from a well-to-do neighborhood where these kinds of cases rarely if ever come to the attention of children's services.) I don't think I really needed to be locked up but it sure couldn't have hurt! Looking back, I'm glad I had my freedom, but obviously there was way too much of it and I'm pleased that I survived that freedom.

I love working with the teenagers. I still surf regularly. I was skateboarding until recently—cement is getting too hard for my old ass. I still have my issues with relationships. I have a hard time being comfortable and successful in long-term close relationships and often don't really want one. I suppose I'd like to get married at some point, if I meet someone who feels like my soul mate. I'm not lonely, except for when I see all that crap around Christmastime that tells me I should be. I don't miss having kids now. I feel like I have 50 of them at all times. I go to a meditation center a couple times weekly where I do chanting programs and meditation. I like turning my attention inward, focusing

One Step Beyond

inside, looking for and finding peace and joy inside of myself, and looking for God inside myself and outside.

I'm actually pretty happy and fulfilled most of the time now. I would suggest therapy to anybody who's looking to feel better. It's a matter of finding a good professional therapist, who's an evolved person, who you feel good to be with.

The bipolar intensity of my teen years is long gone. I look back and sometimes miss the "good old days," then I remember that they were also the bad old days. Nowadays I'm contented and peaceful. I don't have a lot of manic highs and rarely have deep lows. It's weird being middle-aged. All these years seemed to pass so quickly, quicker than I thought when I was young. I don't miss being young because I remember it being so hard. It's exciting being young but you don't know much and you can get your ass kicked so severely.

I wish all of you the best, whether you grew up in the 1980s like me, or in generations before or after. It takes determination, effort and grace to move forward in life without getting knocked off track or completely coming apart. Be good to yourself. Look for happiness within. You can find it there.

Mike Pearson

One Step Beyond

GLOSSARY

1. 1958 Ford Ranchero: cool 50's truck/car mutation. The Chevy version: El Camino.

2. 1966 GT Mustang Fastback: Nice Mustang. Wasn't worth anything until suddenly it became worth a lot.

3. ACDC: Tough Australian rock band. Lead guitar player is like 70 years old and dresses like a school boy.

4. Aerosmith: Rocks and Toys in the Attic albums from the mid 70s were rad; 80s flailing and members almost dying then successful and super corny: Dude Looks Like a Lady.

5. Agro Gyro: Aggressive Gyrating Person.

6. AMC Hornet: Ugly 70s station wagon with terrible handling. Overlooked but as genius as Pinto, Vega and Pacer.

7. April Wine: 70s southern rock band from Canada with too many guitars and a bad name.

8. Area D: a smart school on the Westside. Special, progressive school where you could call your teacher by their first name but had to pass a test to get in.

9. B52's: Fun surfy new wave music from outer space via Georgia. First album rules.

10. Bad Company: Led Zep's little brother who's kind of a wimp. 25% as awesome.

11. Bad Manners: English ska band with a fat singer. Good band.

12. Beemer: BMW.

13. Billy Idol: Early punk/pop. "White Wedding" – awesome song.

14. Billy Joel: Earnest piano man from Long Island. "You had to be a big shot didn't ya!"

15. Black Flag: Top echelon of hardcore punk, or any punk. One of my faves. Early and from South Bay.

16. Blondie: Debbie Harry used to be really hot. Really hot. Punk/disco/new wave/rap. Did I mention that she was really hot.

17. Bob Crane: Sex addict star of Hogan's Heroes, murdered in a motel room. My dad was his agent for a bit. I met him.

18. Boston: 1970s stadium hesher rock. Had a good-time party singer who killed himself. First band to use one million guitar tracks.

19. Bow Wow Wow: Hot, half-naked, 14 year old girl singer with a Mohawk, tribal punk with a Bo Diddley beat. Put together by Malcolm McClaren, manager of the Sex Pistols.

20. Boy George: Was a cute girl who became a fat middle-aged man, male-escort torturer, in jail.

21. Brand Nubian: New hot young babe.

22. Brando: Young Marlon Brando. Cool, young, sexy guy. Classic. Became morbidly obese, old and strange, kissing Larry King.

23. Buster Keaton: Great comedian from the silent movies.

One Step Beyond

24. Camp Josepho: Scary cool hiking spot in a Brentwood canyon. American Nazi's had high hopes for it, but it didn't pan out.

25. Carlos Castaneda: Nerd scholar who took mescaline in the early 60s with an old Indian and had his mind blown into an alternative universe. The book Tales of Power rules.

26. Change Trickster: It's happened to anyone who has worked behind a cash register; bamboozles you to give the wrong change back.

27. Cheap Trick: Had to be there to appreciate it. Great 70s power-pop rock band. Early new wave, in a way.

28. Chuck Biscuits: Kick Ass punk drummer from DOA and other awesome punk bands. One of the best. Played in Black Flag and Circle Jerks.

29. Circle Jerks: Hardcore punk band. Name comes from guys jerking off in a circle with other guys. Keith Morris, first singer from Black Flag, left and formed this band.

30. Clint Eastwood: Man With No Name, Dirty Harry. Classic American bad-ass.

31. Dead Kennedys: Great early San Francisco punk band. So San Francisco. Lead singer named after a popular gelatin dessert and a secessionist state in south-eastern Nigeria.

32. Def Leppard: English new wave heavy metal, girl hair, torn jeans, drummer lost an arm in a car accident and they kept him anyway. Good friends.

33. DOA: Dead On Arrival. Killer Canadian punk band. Singer named Joey Shithead. Tim Blaines' favorite band.

34. Dodge Charger: Gnarly late 60s American muscle car. 8 miles per gallon. You don't see these anymore. Hidden in rich peoples' garages now.

35. Doobie: a joint, jay, marijuana cig, spleef, blunt.

36. Eddie Money: New York Cop who grew his hair and became a rock star.

37. Eight Ball: Mod band from Santa Monica.

38. Enduro: Street legal dirt motorcycle.

39. EP: Extended Play album. Falls between a single and a full album, approx 4 songs. More than 2 songs, less than 10.

40. Fatal Attraction: Movie where Glenn Close got obsessed with Michael Douglas and boiled his bunny. Once she did that you really began to squirm.

41. Fear: Great punk band, excellent musicians, awesome singer, very unpolitically correct.

42. Flipper: Art noise band. They kind of sucked but were good in theory.

43. Flock Of Seagulls: Singer had hair that looked like a flock of seagulls.

44. Foghat: English 70s band that sounded American. Fool for the City. Loved them in the late 70s and loved to hate them in the early 80s. Slowride.

45. Foreigner: see Foghat. "Cold as Ice" and "Double Vision" were bitchen'.

46. Gary Numan: Euro-synth. The very beginning of MTV, looked like Bowie.

One Step Beyond

47. Geza X and The Mommy Men: Trippy L.A. punk. Artsy and truly weird, used a head set before anyone. Geza X was a freak. Producer of many great early punk records.

48. Glitcher: Someone who's all confused and shit.

49. GQ: Gentleman's Quarterly. Professional preppy people who go to work to pay for nice clothes.

50. Green Day: 3rd generation Bay Area punk rock. Helped bring punk to the masses. People like them but say they don't. Billie Joe is the modern Billy Joel, but far cooler.

51. Greener: Stoned hippie heshers who hung out at the Village Green in Palisades Village.

52. Greg Kihn Band: Not the best new wave. Thin ties, checked jackets with big shoulder pads.

53. Grueler: Someone who gruels you, wants something from you, in your face, someone to avoid. Similar to agro gyro but often more bothersome.

54. Haircut 100: Effeminate effervescent new wave music that girls loved so guys thought it was cool and would play it in surf shops. "Love Plus One."

55. Hamilton High: A school that seemed to us like it was in east L.A., but it was still on the West Side.

56. Heaven 17: See Haircut 100.

57. Hesher: Long-haired stoned rockers who couldn't let go of the 70s, until the 90s when they finally got into the 80s, but not the new wave, the rock.

58. Hillbilly: Poor country people. To really qualify you should live in the hills.

59. Hollywood Palladium: Big Los Angeles dance and concert hall that's been around since 1940. Started with Frank Sinatra. Later Grateful Dead, Zep, etc. Then Black Flag, Siouxsie, Bad Religion, etc. Many punk shows put on by Goldenvoice in the early 80s.

60. Hoovering: Vacuuming up big lines of cocaine into your nose '80s style.

61. Human League: "Don't You Want Me Baby," first new wave song to be played on rock station KMET but by then it was too late. KMET died, KROQ rose up.

62. Invasion of the Body Snatchers: Great Sci Fi movie made at least three times. 1979 version was my fave.

63. Iron Maiden: Heavy anthemic metal with lots of important doubled guitar parts. Cute monster album covers.

64. James Dean: Young troubled realistic actor from the 50s who died in a car crash at his peak.

65. Johnny Rotten: Singer of the Sex Pistols. One of the first, one of the best.

66. Joy Division: Early suicidal death rock, droning, depressive. Critics find it to be important. I get bored.

67. Kanan Dume: A canyon road up in Malibu where the motorcyclists go up and come down. They visit "The Rock Store" to eat and talk motos.

68. KMET: Classic rock station that died because it didn't change with times. Was cutting-edge counterculture in the 60s, then became stale and irrelevant.

One Step Beyond

69. Led Zeppelin: Heavy, awesome, moody hard rock band. One of my top faves. They broke up when their alcoholic drummer died of asphyxiation from barfing.

70. Lords Of The New Church: Gothy New Wave. "Open your eyes see the lies right in front of you!"

71. Lynyrd Skynyrd: The kings of 1970s southern rock. Great players, world's best bar band. but songs were often long and self indulgent except when you're drunk and smooching on some fine young thang. "Play Freebird again!"

72. Mac Guard: Minimum-wage private police for rich people. Sometimes they are not around when you need them, sometimes they are around when you don't want them to be, sometimes they go crazy and kill people.

73. Magnolia Thunderpussy: Good prog punk band from my brother's grade. Could have been a contender. Were set to be on Black Flag's SST Records but went to college instead. Boo.

74. Martha Quinn: Cute "VJ" video jockey from early MTV.

75. Michael Jackson: King of Pop. Blew his wad on Thriller. Brought blacks and whites together and probably men and boys too.

76. Missing Persons: Early 80s synth rock. What are "Words" for? "Walking in L.A." "Destination Unknown."

77. Mod: Cool in early 60s then the early 80s. Mod-ska new waver kids, stylish dress, On Club in L.A.. Revived by The Jam, etc, in late 70s early 80s. Fun as hell. Dancing!

78. Molly Hatchet: The opposite of Mod. Multiple guitar southern rock. Like Skynyrd's nasty little brother who might rape your sister. 1979's Flirtin' with Disaster was played too much on KMET.

79. Murphy's Ranch: See Camp Josepho; Murphy's was the earlier name.

80. Narc: Narcotics agent or someone who will tell on you and get you in so much trouble.

81. New Wave: Punk Rock and New Wave are brother and sister. Punk can be harsh. New Wave is friendly, cute and bubbly and so much fun. New Wave is the cool younger sister of disco by a different dad.

82. Nirvana: Punk "grunge" band hit a nerve with Teen Spirit and became gigantic. Cobain had a grueling wife, couldn't handle fame and became a terrible drug addict and killed himself.

83. Nutrition: The time at school where you hang out for 20 minutes at 10:30 am and eat sweet buns and drink chocolate milk.

84. Offspring: An Orange County punk band that got huge in the 90s. MTV hits like "Come Out and Play."

85. Oingo Boingo: Fun energetic new wave band that had great professional musicians, drummers, horn players, etc, and did killer live shows. Could be irritating due to spasmatic music that inspires seizures. Singer Danny Elfman later tried to do every Hollywood movie soundtrack.

86. One Step Beyond: Classic Madness dance song.

One Step Beyond

87. Ozzy: Now we all know Ozzy. I liked him better when I didn't know him so well. He used to seem like he might kill you. Now he seems like he might kill you but by accident.

88. Pali: Pacific Palisades High School. Now a Charter School, whatever that is.

89. Paul Revere: Public junior high school for Westside kids. Used to be grades 7 through 9. Opened in 1955. I was there along with 2500 kids or so in the late 70s. Great banks for skateboarding. Famous big "Blackie" bank as seen in Dogtown and old surf movies. Dozens of yellow buses took us there. All rules broken. Too many kids, not at all manageable by the adults. Like the movie Dazed and Confused. Weed was smoked on the horticulture hill. Didn't learn much of what they tried to teach me.

90. PCH: Pacific Coast Highway.

91. Phone Booth: Please tell me you know what a phone booth is! Before cell phones? It was like a glass booth with a pay phone in it?

92. Pinto: Bad car that would blow up at times when struck from behind.

93. Plymouth Road Runner: Gnarly 70s muscle car, like a Charger. You don't see them anymore. The road runner from the cartoon was the emblem.

94. Plymouth Scamp: a 70s economy car that still wasted a shitload of gas.

95. Preppy: Ivy-league-style collegy, smarty pants people, Yuppies wearing Lacoste polo style shirts with collars up, a lot of pink in 1980. They were going places, upwardly

mobile. We should get some coke! James Spader was an evil one.

96. Psychedelic Furs: New wave punk pop band. "Love My Way" – a great song.

97. Punk Rock: Look it up on Wikipedia. I'm so punk I refuse to explain it. Cuz if I did, then it would cease to be punk and I would be a poseur.

98. Rambo: Sylvester Stallone kicked some major ass for our country in the 80s. Hippies called him a baby killer. But the reality was those babies needed to be killed.

99. Riviera Country Club: Fancy pants country club in Brentwood, right near Paul Revere Junior High. I believe OJ was the only African American they let in. Go figure.

100. Roach: the end of a joint. Why throw them away when you can smoke them? But watch out, you might burn your fingers. Buy a roach clip at Licorice Pizza.

101. Robert Smith: Singer for The Cure. Great early new wave punk band. Started in 76.

102. Rock Store: Place to eat and hang out when you ride motorcycles in the Santa Monica Mountains, east Malibu.

103. Rocky – Sylvester Stallone kicked some major ass for this country in the 70s and 80s. The Italian Stallion. Rocky spawned five sequels. The first movie was great.

104. Santa Monica High: the high school just south of the Palisades. SAMO had great skaters and surfers, like Jay Adams and Tony Alva. SAMO had actors like the Estevezes, Rob Lowe, Sean and Chris Penn. SAMO seemed cooler and

One Step Beyond

tougher than Pali. Santa Monica was gritty back then. Dogtown.

105. The Selecter: Cool English mod band with black woman singer, late 70s, Good songs: "The Missing Words," "Too Much Pressure."

106. Sex Pistols: 1975 and 1976 UK, start of punk rock. Took the Ramones and tweaked it to be more insane, dangerous and amazing. One great album. Ahead of its time. US couldn't handle it, didn't understand it, and blew it off. "Play Freebird, man!"

107. Shadoe Stevens: Fred Rated of Federated Electronic Stores commercials in the 80s. Had hair like Farah Fawcett but he had a beard. To me not cute. Before cell phones he had to pull in and talk in our phone booth at the gas station. See phone booth.

108. Shower Of Smegma: Young punk band with my brother's little friends. Killer for 13 year olds.

109. Ska: Mods like ska. Originally from Jamaica, precursor to rocksteady and reggae. Two Tone label in the late 70s fused ska, rocksteady, reggae, punk and pop. Hot bands in 70s Two Tone revival were Bodysnatchers, English Beat, The Selecter, The Specials, Madness, Bad Manners. That's what we were into.

110. Skanking: Cool fast mod-ska dancing. Elbows out.

111. Social Distortion: Early OC punk band. Mommy's Little Monster album was big in the early 80s.

112. Spirit Catcher: Some crazy ghost shit up at Camp Josepho that would like to steal your soul.

113. Steve Miller: Earthy 70s rock. "Fly Like an Eagle" makes me feel like a stoned 6th grader whenever I hear it. He had a new wave song, "Abracadabra," in the early 80s.

114. Styx: Too much, man! That is so cheesy! "Come Sail Away" ... "Lady" ... and "Mr. Roboto!"

115. Suburban Lawns: Su Tissue was the singer. So punk, weird, new wave and crazy. Art weirdos. The song "I'm a Janitor" sounds like "Oh my genitals." Genius.

116. Ted Nugent: What a Hesher—What a Master Hesher! Good music when you're 14 and stoned and wish you could play guitar like that and are at Laserium and want to fight or break something and take a piss on a wall.

117. The Canyon: Santa Monica Canyon. If you're afraid to say you're from the Palisades due to embarrassment from it being so rich, you can say I'm from Santa Monica Canyon which doesn't help much.

118. The Cars: Great early new wave band from the late 70s and early 80s. Let the "Good Times Roll."

119. The Clash: Highly respected, highly respected. Early punk but then they started playing different styles.

120. The Crowd: Early L.A. punk.

121. The Cure: See Robert Smith. Great band. They were cutting edge.

122. The Dickies: Great when you're a little dude, hilarious vulgar cartoonish loud ripping punk.

123. The Doors: Almost punk before punk in a way. Dark and cool. Doors are an awesome L.A. band.

One Step Beyond

124. The Eagles: They give me that peaceful easy feeling that makes me want to hurt someone.

125. The English Beat: They were great. Mod Ska. I think the singer, Dave Wakeling, now lives in SM canyon.

126. The Exploited: UK punk. Big Mohawks. Tough.

127. The Germs: Hardcore, art, weird, suicidal, really weird band. Did they suck or were they great? I'll go with ... great.

128. The Jam: 70s mod and punky. Cool.

129. The Jetty: Used to be a mile long wharf when they were considering Palisades as the Port of L.A. Long Beach became port of L.A. and we would surf off what was left of the Wharf. Nice rights.

130. The Osmonds: So sickening I can't talk about it.

131. The Outlaws: More putrified southern rock with five guitars. Come on!

132. The Plugz: East L.A. Mexy punk.

133. The Scorpions: German rockers who could sing like big women.

134. The Specials: One of the best mod bands, UK late 70s.

135. The Stray Cats: Rockabilly trio. Standup drummer, stand up bass. Fun music. Good for making out with short-haired new wave chicks.

136. The Talking Heads: Weird, new, different, original. Punk back then.

137. The Untouchables: Great L.A. mod band. Did awesome live shows in early 80s.

138. The Weirdo's: Early bizarre art school punk band. Original. One of L.A.'s first punk bands, if not the first. Covered themselves with food. I had never seen anything like it. Blew my mind, changed my life.

139. Thomas Dolby: "She Blinded Me With Science!" SCIENCE!

140. Tony Alva: One of the best skateboarders in late 70s. Great style. A founder of aerials and pool riding. Dogtown.

141. Topanga Canyon: Between the Palisades and Malibu. Hippies in the hills. Nice!

142. Toto: Wimpy studio musician rock. Name says it all. I secretly like the song "Africa" though. Please don't tell anyone.

143. Travis Bickle: Robert DeNiro in Taxi Driver. Punk, very scary alienated punk. "Are you talkin' to me?"

144. TSOL: Deathy punk from the OC. Singer, a scary guy who would beat people up for fun, who tried to be a politician.

145. Tucker Carlson: Boyish evil preppie right-wing angry talking guy on TV. Yuck!

146. Tuna Canyon: Canyon in Malibu that likes to catch on fire and flood.

147. UFO: English rock band of the late 70s. Another reason punk was necessary.

148. Van Halen: Gotta love that first album. Valley Rock at its heshing finest. Love it!

One Step Beyond

149. Venice: Just south of Santa Monica. Used to be gritty and super cool. Dogtown. Now it's where the rich rub shoulders with the dirty and psychotic.

150. VJ: Video Jockey.

151. Wacky Packs: Collectible cards in the 70s that were spoofs of products you buy at the market. Fun.

152. Weed: It's weed. Marijuana, man! You dig?

153. Westwood: The town where UCLA is. Fun place to go in the late 70s and get high, watch horror movies, try to pick up girls, and play video games.

154. X: Los Angeles punk band with John Doe and Exene, had Ray Manzarek of the Doors on keyboard. Amazing first album. One of the great L.A. punk bands. Saw them live a lot at 15 and was always blown away.

155. Youth Brigade: Smart punk. Too smart. Makes me feel like I'm learning something.

156. Z Channel: The beginning of cable TV. A brown box with push buttons and a cord. R Rated Movies. Sophisticated.

Made in the USA
Charleston, SC
16 March 2010